MEETING
[GOD]
in
Scripture

Entering the
NEW TESTAMENT

MEETING
[GOD]
in
Scripture

Entering the
NEW TESTAMENT

LEADER'S
GUIDE

ANNE CRUMPLER

UPPER
ROOM BOOKS®
NASHVILLE

Cover design: Jade Novak, Anderson Design Group
Cover photo: Shutterstock, iStockPhoto, Photos.com
First printing: 2008

ISBN 978-0-8358-9968-0

Printed in the United States of America

Contents

The daily Bible readings and responses require ten to fifteen minutes a day, and they lead up to and become the starting point for a weekly small-group meeting. This leader's guide includes a process and resources for an introductory meeting and eight weekly meetings of either 45 or 90 minutes. The time for the introductory meeting may vary, depending on how many persons attend and how many community-building activities you include.

Each element of the session has a suggested time frame for a group size of nine. A larger group will be unable to complete the activities in the suggested time. If you attempt to discuss in the whole group rather than in smaller groups of three, time will not allow completion of the activities. Therefore, we strongly encourage you to limit each group to no more than nine persons and to discuss in groups of three. For a larger group, you will need to reduce the time spent on each element or omit a portion from the session plan.

In the introductory meeting, you will present the approach, process, and content of the remaining sessions. (If your group has completed the sessions in *Meeting God in Scripture: Entering the Old Testament*, the introductory session need not be repeated.) The primary difference between this resource and traditional Bible studies is its spiritual formation approach. To many participants, this approach may seem a dramatic departure from the analytical, left-brain methods that often characterize Bible study. Therefore, the introductory meeting will acquaint participants with the difference between formational and informational reading of the Bible. Meetings in the 90-minute format will include group *lectio divina* (contemplation of and individual response to scripture) in each session; the 45-minute format does *not* include group *lectio* each week. This accounts for the time difference between the two formats. Detailed directions for leading *lectio divina* follow this introduction. They will help you guide the group, and you may also use this information to create a computer presentation to aid your teaching.

Customizing the 90-minute Format for Your Group

The first 90-minute session includes get-acquainted activities, an introduction to *lectio divina*, and a group exploration of a scripture passage (EXPLORING THE WORD). Each session (after the introductory session) includes these components:

- Opening
- Interacting with the Word (in triads)
- Exploring the Word (group activity)
- Engaging the Word (*lectio divina*, 90-minute format only)
- Closing

At the end of this guide you will find short introductions to the books of the New Testament, written from a spiritual formation perspective. To prepare to lead each week, read the introductions to the books of the Bible you and participants will study that week. Reading the article "What Is Spiritual Formation?" (page 85) will ready you for the introductory session's exploration activity. Two additional articles, "Meeting God in Service" and "Meeting God in Everyday Life" will give you valuable background information as you lead this study.

Preparing the Meeting Space

The activities in this study aim to involve participants on sensory and affective levels. A welcoming and worshipful atmosphere serves to reinforce those experiences. You may set up a worship center on a small table, using seasonal decorations that change weekly. Or you may develop a worship center with a Christ candle, a cross, and other symbols. A group member may have special gifts for creating such worship arrangements. During the introductory session, ask for volunteers who would prepare the worship center weekly.

Music adds greatly to the sessions. If you cannot lead singing, ask for a volunteer from the group to help with music/singing during opening and closing worship and prayer times. Compile a list of appropriate songs from the songbooks and hymnals available in your meeting place, and give these to the music leader before the first session. You may want to use the same hymn, chorus, or song to begin and end a session, so that you need to choose only eight.

Each session will include conversation in groups of three about the week's readings and entry-point responses, so a setting in which chairs move easily from a circle arrangement (for OPENING and the large-group discussion of INTERACTING WITH THE WORD) into triads (for small-group discussion) would be advantageous.

When sessions include handouts, placing these on chairs or tables before participants arrive reduces confusion and creates a more peaceful atmosphere. If you plan to use a computer presentation, check it out before each session to reduce technological problems, confusion, and wasted time.

Looking Ahead: Supplies/Special Arrangements

All sessions: Always have on hand, newsprint or whiteboard and markers, extra Bibles, paper and writing utensils, name tags.

Intro session: The introductory session calls for modeling clay or play dough for each participant. Copies of "Obstacles to Hearing God in Scripture" (page 15) and "Informational and Formational Reading" (page 16) for each participant.

Session 2:   Paper on which to journal, pencils or pens.

Session 3:   You will need a variety of pictures of the Crucifixion and of the women at the tomb. Bring these to show to the group, or copy or print a picture of the Resurrection onto a transparency sheet. Overhead projector is optional depending on your choice of medium. Newsprint, markers, paper on which to journal, pencils or pens.

Session 4:   For Exploring the Word, set up prayer centers. Copy instructions for each center from this leader's guide. Supplies needed for prayer centers include the following: center 1, newsprint and markers; center 2, colored pencils, crayons, unlined paper; center 4, lined paper and pens.

Session 5:   You will need recent copies of newspapers and news magazines, construction paper, and clear tape.

Session 6:   Copies of Exploring the Word reflection (page 44) for all participants; lined paper, pencils or pens.

Session 7:   You will need a CD player and a CD of Handel's *Messiah*, paint, brushes, and paint shirts or smocks.

Session 8:   Make a copy of the prayer quotations handout for each participant. Provide crayons and colored pencils and extra blank paper for Exploring the Word exercise.

Leading Lectio Divina in Groups (for 90-minute sessions)

Lectio divina is a Latin phrase often translated as "spiritual reading" or "holy reading." But for the first fifteen hundred years of the Christian church, people learned and absorbed the words and stories of scripture by *hearing* them read. Scrolls and books were rare, and most people could not read. Personal copies of the Bible in the language of ordinary life were not available until long after the invention of the printing press in the mid-1400s, and even then only to the wealthy. So when we hear scripture being read, we sit in company with the first saints who listened to hear God's personal word to them through the words of the Bible.

If you have never led *lectio divina* in a small group, the process outlined here may seem too simple to be effective. Please trust the approach. In just a few sessions you will see God at work as participants grow in their eagerness and ability to hear God speak to them through the words of scripture. Those who tested this resource emphasized that the group reflection on scripture was an invaluable part of the design. The time investment is worth the return for the participants. For more background on *lectio divina*, read "Meeting God in Scripture" (page 103).

Lectio divina is based on hearing a passage of scripture read several times. Using the directions below, you will guide group members in listening, reflecting in silence, talking with others, and praying in response to what they have heard. Allowing silence may be the most difficult part of the process for both leader and participants. Don't rush the silence; use a watch with a second hand to be sure you allow ample time for each step.

Preparing the Group to Listen

Before the first session of *lectio divina*, you may want to reflect together on "Obstacles to Hearing God in Scripture" (page 15) as group members think about all the things we do instead of listening—analyzing, classifying, and so on. The first two steps in the *lectio* process may be the most demanding because they require listening and silence. In the first step, you will invite group members to listen for a word or phrase from the Bible passage you read and to consider it in silence. The second tough step comes when you direct them to repeat *only* that word or phrase within their small group. They speak it aloud without comment or elaboration.

We are so accustomed to analyzing, to stepping back from scripture to *think about* what it means, that we often do not listen to the words themselves. For instance, if we read aloud the story of the persistent widow from Luke 18:1-8, some people will think and say within their group the word *perseverance*. But that word does not appear in the passage. That word and others like it (*compassion, mercy, faith*) are thoughts about the passage, and they reflect our analysis rather than the words we actually heard. Try to help group members realize that they are to listen for a word or phrase that occurs in the passage, not come up with a word to *describe* the passage. They are not to step back to analyze or categorize the reading.

Before you begin, invite group members to sit in groups of three, to become comfortable, and to prepare for a time of listening to scripture. Tell them that they will be hearing a passage of scripture—the same passage—read several times and that each reading will be followed by silence for reflection. Ask them to trust you to guide them through the process. Suggest that they give themselves fully to hearing the scripture—not reading along in their own Bibles but listening.

On the third reading, a group member will read the passage aloud so participants will hear it at least once in a voice other than yours. Ask for a volunteer to do this before beginning. Read the passage from the same translation each time to avoid distracting people by differences between the translations. You may want to photocopy from your Bible the page containing each session's *lectio divina* passage and mark the reading to make the change of readers less intrusive and to be sure the same translation is used. Tell the participants that the small groups will not be "reporting" to the entire body in any way and that what they say within their smaller groups will remain private.

The Process for Group *Lectio Divina*

STEP ONE: (first-stage reading) Tell the group members that you will read the passage twice, once to orient them to its overall content and then again, more slowly, so that they can listen for a word or phrase that stops them or gets their attention. Read the passage aloud, twice.

In the silence, repeat your word or phrase to yourself and reflect on it.

Allow one to two minutes of silence. (*Time this step so you do not rush.*)

STEP TWO: **Within your group, repeat the word or phrase that attracted you—without comment, summary, or analysis. (Or you may pass.)**

STEP THREE: (second-stage reading) Ask group members to listen as you read the passage again, slowly, being open to how it connects to them. (Tell them that their word or phrase may or may not be the same one on this reading as during the first reading.)

In silence, consider how your word or phrase connects to your life right now—a situation, a feeling, a possibility.

Allow three minutes of silence for reflection.

STEP FOUR: (At this point, tell the group that participants may always choose not to speak by saying "pass" when their turn comes.)

In your groups, take a few minutes each to tell about the connection you sense between your life and your word or phrase. (Or you may pass.)

Ask the person closest to you in each group to be the first speaker.

STEP FIVE: (third-stage reading) Ask the alternate reader to read the passage again, slowly. Invite group members to listen during this reading for an invitation from God for the next few days:

In the silence, consider what invitation you hear from God. Be open to a sensory impression, an image, a song, a fragrance.

Allow three minutes of silence for reflection.

STEP SIX: Ask group members to ponder in silence the invitation they heard. Allow several minutes of silence.

STEP SEVEN: Invite each person to speak about the invitation he or she senses from God for his or her life in the next few days:

In your groups, allow each person to tell about the invitation he or she heard. (Or you may pass.)

This time, have the person farthest from you to begin. This is an important step in the process, so allow ample time for each person to speak. Watch the groups; check to see which are finishing up, which need more time. Do not rush the process.

STEP EIGHT: Invite persons to pray for each other, one by one in turn, within their smaller groups. Ask each one to pray for the person to his or her right. The group members can decide whether they will pray aloud or silently.

Pray for each other to be empowered to respond to the invitations you heard. (You may pray silently or aloud.)

Remind participants to remain silent when their group finishes praying, since other groups may still be in prayer. When all have finished praying, say "amen" to end the process.[1]

You may want to debrief this experience of *lectio divina* by asking the group as a whole to comment on it: What worked for them? What was difficult about this way of responding to scripture? Have they been led through this process before, and, if so, what was different, better, or worse about it this time? This would be a good time to mention that everyone responds differently to the various ways of exploring scripture and that there is no expected outcome.

Obstacles to Hearing God in Scripture

Common obstacles:

- thinking/talking about scripture

- classifying

- comparing

- describing

- explaining

- looking for "the lesson" rather than listening to scripture:

  the actual words that are there

  the emotions we feel

  the connections we make

  the memories that arise

Informational and Formational Reading

Reading for information is an integral part of teaching and learning. But reading is also concerned with listening for the special guidance, for the particular insight, for your relationship with God. What matters is the attitude of mind and heart.

Informational Reading

1. Informational reading is concerned with covering as much material as possible and as quickly as possible.

2. Informational reading is linear— seeking an objective meaning, truth, or principle to apply.

3. Informational reading seeks to master the text.

4. In informational reading, the text is an object out there for us to control.

5. Informational reading is analytical, critical, and judgmental.

6. Informational reading is concerned with problem solving.

Formational Reading

1. Formational reading is concerned with small portions of content rather than quantity.

2. Formational reading focuses on depth and seeks multiple layers of meaning in a single passage.

3. Formational reading allows the text to master the student.

4. Formational reading sees the student as the object to be shaped by the text.

5. Formational reading requires a humble, detached, willing, loving approach.

6. Formational reading is open to mystery. Students come to the scripture to stand before the Mystery called God and to let the Mystery address them.

Adapted from information in *Shaped by the Word: The Power of Scripture in Spiritual Formation*, rev. ed., by M. Robert Mulholland Jr. (Nashville, TN.: Upper Room Books, 2000), 49–63. Used by permission of Upper Room Books.

Shaped by God

Preparing for the introductory session: Read the article "What Is Spiritual Formation?" (leader's guide, page 85) and the article "Reading Scripture Devotionally" in the participant's workbook (page 11). Look over the chart comparing informational and formational approaches to reading scripture (page 16). Make copies of this chart to give to group members. If you plan to lead *lectio divina* in each session, be sure to provide copies of "Obstacles to Hearing God in Scripture" (page 15).

Note ideas from the articles that you feel are important. Read through the plan for the introductory session until you feel comfortable leading it, especially the reading from Genesis and the reflection on it. You will need to tailor this session to fit your time frame. An alternate approach to the introductions is provided. Other places to save time might include passing out materials without a great deal of discussion.

Materials Needed

- Worship center (Christ candle, and a means to light it)
- Participant's workbooks. Since group members will be writing or drawing in their books as part of the daily reflection, each person will need his or her own copy.

- Name tags and markers
- Modeling clay or play dough for each participant
- Extra Bibles for those who may not have brought theirs
- Copies (one for each participant) of "Informational and Formational Reading" (page 16) and "Obstacles to Hearing God in Scripture" (page 15)

Opening (5 minutes)

Welcome persons as they arrive. Distribute the participant's workbooks as part of your greeting, and invite folks to browse through them until the session begins.

Light the candle and tell the group you light it as a reminder that the One who created light—and us—is present with us in this study to shed light on all we will do.

Read Genesis 1:1-3*a*. Invite the group members to mention aloud other good things that they have experienced this week. Offer a prayer of gratitude for all God's good gifts to us, especially the gift of being able to study scripture together.

Sing a hymn or chorus.

Building Community (20 minutes)

Welcome participants to the study. Explain that they'll receive more information about what to expect during the coming weeks, later in the session, after they get to know one another better.

Introductions: Invite group members to pair off by finding a person they do not know or the person they know least well in the group. Tell them that, after conversation, they will introduce each other to the group. Give the pairs six minutes to get to know each other (signal when three minutes has passed). Suggest nonthreatening questions to ask, such as how they came to attend this church, where they live, where they went to school, what denomination they grew up in. *Add one specific question:* What is one fact about you that probably no one else in the room knows? After six minutes, invite the pairs to introduce each other to the rest of the group based on their conversation. Give the speakers one or two minutes each for the introductions, depending on the size of the group.

Alternate introductions for 45-minute session (10 minutes): Have persons introduce themselves. Give people one minute to say whatever they want about themselves, including one fact about them that no one in the room knows.

Establishing a Group Agreement (10 minutes)

Most small groups operate with an agreement that includes points such as these:

Presence: Attend each meeting unless serious reasons keep you away.

Prayer: Between meeting times, group members pray for one another and for the group's endeavors together.

Preparation: Group members make the daily readings and exercises a priority, doing them as diligently as life allows.

Participation: Group members will participate honestly and openly in the activities of the sessions.

Confidentiality: What is said within the group remains in the group. Members will not discuss outside the group anything others say within this setting.

Courtesy: Group members will listen to one another with respect and without interrupting or engaging in side conversations. When opinions differ, group members will not attempt to persuade anyone to any point of view but will listen for what God may be saying in the differences.

Post the words *presence, prayer, preparation, participation, confidentiality,* and *courtesy* on newsprint or a board. Mention what each means for this group and ask if folks want to accept these definitions or add to or modify them. You may want to display reminders of your group's agreement in the meeting room each time you gather.

Introducing the Study (20 minutes)

Be sure all participants have a copy of the workbook.

Explain that this study of the Bible will probably differ from other studies folks may have participated in. There will be no memorizing or outlining. Have participants open their workbooks to page 26, to the entry point related to session 2, day 2. Give them time to read the suggested guided response to Mark 10:17-31. Ask, "Based on looking at this process, how does this way of studying the Bible compare to other studies you have participated in?" List the responses on newsprint.

Next, direct the attention of the group to the article "Reading Scripture Devotionally" (page 11, participant's workbook). Give the members time to read the article. After five minutes, check to see if everyone is finished and allow more time as necessary. When they have completed the reading, ask them to compare the article's ideas to their responses listed on the newsprint. Where do their ideas echo the article? Where do their ideas differ from those in the article? What questions or concerns did the article raise for them? Respond to questions. If you don't have an answer to someone's concern, invite group members to respond.

Explain that the ideas in the article shape this study. This study will not attempt to survey the entire New Testament. Each day participants will read a portion of scripture. Then they will read again, looking closely at one verse or a few verses from the passage. They will respond to the verse or verses by following the process suggested in each "entry point." Each day's reading and activity will take only ten to fifteen minutes to complete.

The "starred" entry point: One of each week's five entry points has two stars alongside the title. (Direct them to page 21: session 1, day 3, to show them a starred article.) Ask participants to make time to do the starred activity each week even if they are too crunched for time to do them all, because the starred activity will be part of the weekly group meeting.

Direct their attention to the section of the introduction titled "If You Want to Do More: Keeping a Spiritual Journal" (page 9) and talk about keeping a journal. Ask if any in the group have kept a journal. If so, invite these persons to tell the group the benefits they received from the practice. Emphasize that journals are private, and no one will be asked to reveal anything he or she has written.

Exploring the Word (15 minutes)

Distribute the modeling clay or play dough. Encourage group members to begin manipulating the clay, shaping and reshaping it.

Explain that you will read some passages from Genesis to the group and you want them to work the clay as they listen. Ask them to notice the temperature of the clay, its pliability, its weight, and then to begin to knead it, gently and firmly. Then ask them to think of a shape and to begin to form the clay into that shape while you read.

Read aloud Genesis 1:1-31 and 2:1-8. Read Genesis 2:1-8 a second time, more slowly. When you finish reading, allow folks several minutes to finish their clay creations. Then direct them to the entry point for Genesis 1:1-31; 2:1-8 (page 15, participant's workbook). Ask them to take two minutes to write responses as suggested in the entry point.

Invite group members to talk about what they think the term *spiritual formation* means in light of working with the clay. Remind them that the Bible readings and entry-point responses in this study provide spiritual-formation opportunities by helping us attend to God's work in our lives as we become conformed to the image of Christ.

Discussion: Formational Versus Informational Reading (15 minutes)

Distribute copies of the chart comparing the two ways of reading the Bible and other Christian resources. Talk about the entries on the chart and help group members compare the two approaches. Point out that our educational system concentrates on helping students develop left-brain, analytical skills and often presents education as a linear process focusing on cognitive abilities. For example, ask participants to think about the difference between attitudes about art classes and math classes in an average school or about our constant quantifying (grades, reports, assessments) rather than relational focus in educating. We will be approaching scripture as an opportunity to encounter God and learn about ourselves and one another.

Closing (5 minutes)

Invite group members to voice their wishes and hopes about this course and the group's time together.

Pray, offering to God all the hopes and wishes expressed and asking for God's help in listening and responding with heart, soul, mind, and strength.

Ask for volunteers who might be willing to assist in music selection and singing or those who might enjoy helping set up the worship center each week.

Preparing for Session 1

- Complete the daily readings and entry-point responses in the participant's workbook.

- Read the introduction to the Gospel of Matthew.

- Write and post the questions you will focus on in Interacting with the Word.

- Review the process for leading *lectio divina* until you feel comfortable using it, and photocopy and mark the scripture passage for the alternate reader.

- Provide name tags and markers.

- Prepare materials for the worship center.

- Have paper, crayons or markers available

Blessed in the

Promises of God

NOTE: All meeting outlines are for 90-minute sessions; if you are using this study in a 45-minute session, you will need to omit the *lectio divina* experience.

Have name tags and markers available every week.

Opening (5 minutes)

Light the candle. Tell the group that you do so as a reminder of God's presence in the world and in our lives.

Propose that the members be thinking about one or two words that describe their relationship with God in Jesus Christ as the group sings the first several verses of "Open My Eyes, That I May See" or "Send Your Word."

Ask participants to say aloud the words that describe their relationship with God in Jesus Christ.

Invite the group to sing together the last two verses of the chosen hymn.

Interacting with the Word (15 minutes)

Begin by allowing participants a couple of minutes to review their comments and daily responses to the Bible readings in their participant's workbook.

Below are several questions the smaller groups (triads) might use when discussing each week's Bible reading and responses. Choose two of the questions for discussion this week and gauge the group's response to them. You may use the same questions each week or vary them. Write the questions you'll be using on a board or flip chart.

Encourage group members to listen for God in each person's words. Remind everyone to allow each group member time to respond to a question before the group moves on to the next.

Some possible questions:

- What scripture reading and accompanying entry point did you find most relevant to your life?
- What scripture reading and entry-point activity most surprised you?
- What did you learn through the week's readings?
- What insight did you connect with your life?
- What persons or ideas touched on this week would you like to know more about?
- What reading most challenged you?
- What questions do you have about the week's readings?
- What relationships do you see differently due to the week's readings and activities?
- How did your actions or attitudes change in response to the daily Bible readings?

If you prefer, use questions of your own.

Exploring the Word (20 minutes)

This activity builds on the entry point for Matthew 5:1-12.

Jesus walked from town to town preaching the good news of God's kingdom. Like the first people who sat and listened, we take our place in the crowd and hear God's word.

Say: **The Beatitudes reveal several layers of meaning: the beginning of a new covenant with God, a statement of God's promise and a picture of God's kingdom, and a call for**

change. Read the scripture aloud, asking people to be aware of the layers of meaning.

Invite participants to spend a few minutes reflecting on persons in their lives who illustrate the Beatitudes. Read slowly the first half of each beatitude from Matthew 5:3-11 (Blessed are the poor in spirit, blessed are those who mourn, etc.) and ask them to call to mind the names and faces of people they know described by Jesus' words and to hold those persons in prayer.

After a few moments of silence, read the entirety of Matthew 5:1-11 asking the participants to consider these same people living out the blessing Jesus has for them.

After a few moments of silence, read the scripture a final time asking the participants to imagine a community and a world that makes these blessings real.

After a few moments of silence, close by reading Matthew 5:12: "Rejoice and be glad, for your reward is great in heaven."

Ask volunteers to describe the person(s) they saw and how he or she changed as they lived into the Beatitudes. Or provide paper and crayons or makers, and invite each person to draw the person and transformation they envisioned.

Engaging the Word (lectio divina, 45 minutes)

Use the steps outlined for leading group *lectio* to guide the group through contemplation of **Matthew 6:9-15**.

Closing (5 minutes)

Close your time together by asking participants what insights they gained during the session. How did Jesus' teachings deepen or change their relationship with God? Model this by mentioning an insight you had either while preparing or during the session.

Sing a hymn, song, or chorus of trust in God's promises.

Invite the group to say together the Lord's Prayer.

Preparing for Session 2

- Complete the daily readings and entry-point responses in the participant's workbook.

- Read the introduction to the Gospels of Mark and Luke.

- Write and post the questions you will focus on in Interacting with the Word.

- Review the process for leading *lectio divina* until you feel comfortable using it, and photocopy and mark the passage for the alternate reader.

- Prepare materials for the worship center.

- Write on a large sheet of paper: "How do we try to earn eternal life?"

- Have available large sheets of paper and markers.

- Prepare to lead participants through Exploring the Word.

- Provide paper on which to journal, pencils or pens.

- Make one copy of the closing prayer for each participant.

Coming before Christ

As Is

NOTE: All meeting outlines are for 90-minute sessions; if you are using this study in a 45-minute session, you will need to omit the *lectio divina* experience.

Have name tags and markers available every week.

Opening (5 minutes)

Light the candle. Tell the group that you do so as a reminder of God's presence in the world and in our lives.

Ask the members to be thinking about one or two words that describe who they are as the group sings the first several verses of a hymn, song, or chorus about coming before the Lord as we are such as "Come, Sinners, to the Gospel Feast" and "Come, Ye Sinners, Poor and Needy."

Ask participants to say aloud the words that describe who they are.

Invite the group to sing together the closing verses of the chosen hymn.

Interacting with the Word (15 minutes)

Invite participants to form small groups of three people to discuss the week's Bible readings and activities.

Use the same questions as last week or choose new ones from the list. Give time for review of responses in the participant's workbook before the discussion begins. Write the questions you'll be using on a board or flip chart. Once again, encourage group members to listen for God in the responses of others in their small group.

Exploring the Word (20 minutes)

This activity builds on the entry point for Mark 10:17-31.

The story of the rich man puts side by side common understandings of success and salvation with Jesus' love, his call to follow, and ultimately the power of God to save.

Write at the top of a large sheet of paper: "How do we try to earn eternal life?" Invite the group to make a list of common answers to the question, such as, obey the Ten Commandments, be kind, help people, go to church. Ask a volunteer to read Mark 10:27 and ask the group if meeting this list of "requirements" is even possible? What does the scripture mean that "for God all things are possible"? How does this change our list?

Say, **When the rich young man heard what stood between him and eternal life he could not see beyond his wealth to God's possibilities. Take some time to journal about a time when you heard God's call but could not see through your own circumstances to the promise of God. What were your emotions during this time? What actions did you take?**

Ask participants to pair up and discuss their reflections. Suggest they pray for each other that God would bring each of them back to a place of possibility or give him or her a new vision in the midst of present circumstances.

Engaging the Word (lectio divina, 45 minutes)

Use the steps outlined for leading group *lectio* to guide the group through contemplation of **Luke 10:25-37**.

Closing (5 minutes)

Invite the group to say together the following prayer:

God, we see ourselves in the rich young ruler, longing for a life with you, the abundant life available through Jesus Christ. But we also know the temptation to follow our own wisdom and deny your calling. Be patient with us, merciful Lord. Give us clear direction and a willing heart to step out trusting in your possibilities. Amen.

Read aloud a declaration of pardon: **"For mortals it is impossible, but not for God; for God all things are possible." In Christ Jesus, your sins are forgiven. Inherit the promise of eternal life!**

Invite the group to sing a hymn of trust in God, such as, "Amazing Grace" or "Just as I Am, Without One Plea."

Close by praying together the Lord's Prayer.

Preparing for Session 3

- Complete the daily readings and entry-point responses in the participant's workbook.

- Read and review the introductions to the Gospels of Matthew, Mark, Luke, and the book of Acts.

- Write and post the questions you will focus on in Interacting with the Word.

- Review the process for leading *lectio divina* until you feel comfortable using it, and photocopy and mark the passage for the alternate reader.

- Prepare materials for the worship center.

- Have available pictures of the Crucifixion and of the women at the tomb.

- Prepare to lead participants through Exploring the Word.

Encountering Christ in His Death and

Resurrection

NOTE: All meeting outlines are for 90-minute sessions; if you are using this study in a 45-minute session, you will need to omit the *lectio divina* experience.

Opening (5 minutes)

Do *not* light the candle. Tell participants that this session will focus on the crucifixion of Jesus Christ. With his death, the light of God's presence in the world was extinguished.

Propose that members be thinking about one or two words that describe what the crucifixion and resurrection of Jesus means to them as the group sings the first several verses of a hymn such as "Were You There"; "O Sacred Head, Now Wounded"; or "Alas! and Did My Savior Bleed."

Ask participants to say aloud their words.

Invite the group to sing together the closing verses of the chosen hymn.

Interacting with the Word (15 minutes)

Invite participants to form small groups of three people to discuss the week's Bible readings and activities.

Use the same questions as last week or choose new ones from the list. Give time for review of responses in the participant's workbook before the discussion begins. Write the questions you'll be using on a board or flip chart. Once again, encourage group members to listen for God in the responses of others in their small group.

Exploring the Word (20 minutes)

This activity builds on the entry point for Mark 16:1-8.

Have available a variety of pictures of Jesus' crucifixion (one for each participant). Invite each person to choose one. Explain that they may meditate on the image as you read aloud Matthew 27:32-55, followed by several minutes of silence. Break the silence by saying, "On the third day, Jesus rose from the dead!" Ask volunteers to show the images they chose and why. Allow them time to share emotions, questions, and insights from the prayer time.

Display a picture of the women at the tomb. You may find one in an art book, print one from the internet, or display the image using a computer and screen. (Having the picture is optional.) Invite the group to meditate on this image as you read Mark 16:1-8, remembering that these same women were the last ones we heard about in the passage we read from Matthew.

As you finish, ask participants what these women must have experienced between the crucifixion and the resurrection. How difficult must it have been to wrap their minds around the death of their friend and savior, and now his resurrection?

Suggest that they spend some time journaling about a time when they have felt this emotional and spiritual shift in themselves from death to new life. Reflect on what accompanied that shift in their own experience.

While the group is journaling, write the following call and response on newsprint. Call the group back together, light the candle, and invite the group to pray together:

Jesus Christ is risen!
He is risen indeed!

In Jesus Christ, we are forgiven!
Hallelujah!
In Jesus Christ, God gives new life.
Hallelujah! Amen.

Engaging the Word (lectio divina, 45 minutes)

Use the steps outlined for leading group *lectio* to guide the group through contemplation of **2 Corinthians 5:17-20**.

Closing (5 minutes)

Conclude your time together by asking participants what insights they gained during the session. How did their experience of contemplating Jesus' death and resurrection change their relationship with God? How did it affect their understanding of the church?

Invite the group to sing together a hymn such as "Christ the Lord Is Risen Today"; "Thine Be the Glory"; or "Walk On, O People of God."

Invite the group to say responsively:

Jesus Christ is risen!
He is risen indeed!

Preparing for Session 4

- Complete the daily readings and entry-point responses in the participant's workbook.

- Read the introduction to the Gospel of John.

- Write and post the questions you will focus on in Interacting with the Word.

- Review the process for leading *lectio divina* until you feel comfortable using it, and photocopy and mark the passage for the alternate reader.

- Prepare materials for the worship center.

- Create prayer centers for Exploring the Word. Make copies of the instructions for each center. Supplies needed for prayer centers include the following: center 1: newsprint and markers; center 2: colored pencils, crayons, unlined paper; center 4: lined paper and pens.

A New Creation

in Christ

NOTE: All meeting outlines are for 90-minute sessions; if you are using this study in a 45-minute session, you will need to omit the *lectio divina* experience.

Opening (5 minutes)

Light the candle. Tell the group that you do so as a reminder of God's presence in the world and in our lives.

Invite the group members to consider one or two words that articulate their hopes for the world as the group sings together the opening verses of a hymn such as "For the Healing of the Nations" or "Let There Be Light."

Ask participants to say aloud their words.

Invite the group to sing together the closing verses of the chosen hymn.

Interacting with the Word (15 minutes)

Form small groups of three people to discuss the week's Bible readings and responses.

Use the same questions as last week or choose new ones from the list. Give time for review of responses in the participant's workbook before the discussion begins. Write the questions you'll be using on a board or flip chart. Once again, encourage group members to listen for God in the responses of others in their small group.

Exploring the Word (20 minutes)

This exercise builds on the entry point for John 1:1-18.

The first verses of John are a hymn of praise to Jesus Christ.

To help people focus on the theology of John 1:1-18, create these prayer centers. Copy the content and focus of the prayer stations from below and display one at each of five prayer centers around your gathering space.

1. **"In the beginning was the Word" (John 1:1); "Then God said . . . " (Gen. 1:3).**

    The spoken word is powerful. With mere words, God spoke creation into being. John connects Jesus to this power by calling him the "Word" that was present at creation with God. This Word, or *Logos* in Greek (meaning "divine reason"), has the power to link creation to God.

    DIRECTIONS: Write on newsprint the words that hold power for you: quotes, verses, wisdom—or Word—that link you to God.

2. **"In the beginning was the Word, and the Word was with God, and the Word was God. He was in the beginning with God. All things came into being through him, and without him not one thing came into being" (John 1:1-3).**

    Read Genesis 1:1–2:4 and try to imagine Jesus present at creation.

    DIRECTIONS: Now imagine this same Jesus, the Word, growing up as a man in the same creation over three thousand years later. What would have delighted him? What would have pained him?

    Finally, imagine Jesus walking in creation today. What parts of creation would he not recognize? What new things would he delight in?

    Use the art supplies provided to draw an image of creation that delights Jesus today.

3. **"There was a man sent from God, whose name was John. He came as a witness to testify to the light, so that all might believe through him"(John 1:6-7).**

   DIRECTIONS: Read about John the Baptist in Luke 1:76-79; 3:1-22.

4. **"[Jesus] came to what was his own, and his own people did not accept him" (John 1:11).**

   DIRECTIONS: Read about Jesus' reception in Luke 4:16-30.

   Think about modern-day prophets who are still dismissed, ridiculed, or rejected. Are they politicians or pastors or laypeople? Young people or old? Wealthy or poor? Christian, Jewish, or Muslim?

   Write a prayer or a letter of support to one of these leaders.

5. **"From his fullness we have all received, grace upon grace" (John 1:16).**

   DIRECTIONS: Reflect on Jesus' life. Imagine him present at creation; present with Abraham and Sarah, Moses and Miriam, John the Baptist, Mary Magdalene, and Paul and Timothy. Then look for his presence in the lives of Augustine, Martin Luther, John Wesley, Mother Teresa, Martin Luther King Jr., Billy Graham, and Jim Wallis or other saints, modern-day or ancient.

   Give thanks for God's grace poured out through Jesus Christ. Now cup your hands and receive the grace that God offers to you.

Invite people to visit each of the centers to complete suggested activities. When everyone has had time to visit the prayer centers, call the group together and invite responses to the experiences.

Engaging the Word (lectio divina, 45 minutes)

Use the steps outlined for leading group *lectio* to guide the group through contemplation of **John 3:11-21.**

Closing (5 minutes)

Close your time together by asking participants what insights they gained during the session. How did the scripture deepen or change their relationship with God?

Invite the group to sing together a hymn in praise of Jesus Christ and then by saying together the Lord's Prayer.

Preparing for Session 5

- Complete the daily readings and entry-point responses in the participant's workbook.

- Read the introductions to the Gospel of John and First, Second, and Third John.

- Write and post the questions you will focus on in Interacting with the Word.

- Review the process for leading *lectio divina* until you feel comfortable using it, and photocopy and mark the passage for the alternate reader.

- Prepare materials for the worship center.

- Collect newspapers, news magazines, clear tape, construction paper, scissors.

- Write closing prayer on newsprint.

New Life in

Christ

NOTE: All meeting outlines are for 90-minute sessions; if you are using this study in a 45-minute session, you will need to omit the *lectio divina* experience.

Opening (5 minutes)

Light the candle. Tell the group that you do so as a reminder of God's presence in the world and in our lives.

Invite members to think about one or two words that describe the community of faith as the group sings the opening verses of a hymn, song or chorus, such as "Where Charity and Love Prevail" or "Lord, Whose Love Through Humble Service," about the love of Christ expressed in the Christian community.

Ask the participants to say their words aloud.

Close this time by singing together the final verses of the chosen hymn.

Interacting with the Word (15 minutes)

Invite participants to form small groups of three people to discuss the week's Bible readings and exercises.

Use the same questions as last week or choose new ones from the list. Give time for review of responses in the participant's workbook before the discussion begins. Write the questions you'll be using on a board or flip chart. Once again, encourage group members to listen for God in the responses of others in their small group.

Exploring the Word (20 minutes)

This exercise builds on the entry point for 1 John 3:16-18. Listen carefully to this story about radical love.

As she sat in the courtroom waiting her turn to step into the witness box, she relived the entire experience.

She had heard something crash downstairs and crept to the top of the stairs. Voices, she heard voices downstairs! "Not tonight!" the voice in her head protested. It was the first night in years that her husband had had to work all night. She crept back across the wood floorboards into the den, grabbed the phone, hid under the desk, and dialed 9-1-1. She whispered to the operator that there were men in her house. No, she didn't know how many. She stopped midsentence as she heard them coming up the stairs. She told the operator, "They're here."

"Shhhhh . . . ," responded the operator. "It's okay. The police are on their way. Just be quiet now."

Terrified, she had held her breath as the intruders entered the room. In the dark she could see the legs of one of the men, inches from her face as he rummaged through the papers on the desk under which she hid. The next thing she remembered was the police officer kneeling where the intruder had been, assuring her that they were gone and it was safe to come out.

She shuddered there in the seat of the courtroom as she remembered calling her husband and walking together through their now disheveled home, examining the piles of jewelry and trinkets the thieves had planned to take with them and the knives they had left behind as they fled.

She took a deep breath, said a prayer for courage, and walked to the front of the courtroom where she was prepared to give testimony at one of the men's sentencing hearing. She sat down, looked into the blank eyes of this twenty-something young man, and said, "You have taken my home from me. It was the place where I always felt safe and where I kept my family safe. And now it is just a house. But I am here to tell you that I have been praying for you every day since you broke into my home. Everyone here knows that you know exactly where I live; and I want you to know that when you get out of jail, if you have nowhere else to go, you can come to my house. Because if you had come and knocked on my door that night I would have let you in and given you anything you needed. I don't ever want you to have to sit here again because of poor choices you've made. So if you need help when you get out, you can come to my home. Because I will make it a home again."

How do you respond to this story? Is this love or craziness? As a Christian, how can you tell the difference? Where do you see the radical love of Christ being lived in the world?

Provide recent newspapers and news magazines. Ask each person to choose an article and to tape the article to a sheet of construction paper. Collect the articles and redistribute them. Then ask people to read the article they have received and to write on the construction paper one or more answers to the question: In what ways does this article demonstrate God's love or lack of Christian love? What would Jesus have us do in response?

Encourage a time of spoken prayer for each situation raised in the articles. Then close by reading aloud 1 John 3:16-18.

Engaging the Word (lectio divina, 45 minutes)

Use the steps outlined for leading group *lectio* to guide the group through contemplation of **John 14:15-27**.

Closing (5 minutes)

Close your time together by asking participants what insights they gained during the session. How has their relationship with one another and with God deepened or changed?

Sing a hymn, song, or chorus about God's love in Jesus Christ and in the church.

Invite the group to pray together: **God, teach us to love as you love, in Jesus Christ our Lord. Amen.**

Preparing for Session 6

- Complete the daily readings and entry-point responses in the participant's workbook.

- Read the introductions to Romans and First and Second Corinthians.

- Write and post the questions you will focus on in Interacting with the Word.

- Review the process for leading *lectio divina* until you feel comfortable using it, and photocopy and mark the passage for the alternate reader.

- Prepare materials for the worship center.

- Make a copy of the reflection in Exploring the Word for each participant.

- Provide lined paper and pencils or pens for journaling.

Amazing

Grace

NOTE: All meeting outlines are for 90-minute sessions; if you are using this study in a 45-minute session, you will need to omit the *lectio divina* experience.

Opening (5 minutes)

Light the candle. Tell the group that you do so as a reminder of God's presence in the world and in our lives.

Ask the participants to consider words that describe their struggle to do what is right as the group sings together the opening verses of a hymn, song, or chorus of repentance, such as, "Depth of Mercy" or one or two verses of "Sinners, Turn: Why Will You Die."

Encourage participants to say their words aloud.

Sing the closing verses of the chosen hymn.

Interacting with the Word (15 minutes)

Invite participants to form small groups of three people to discuss the week's Bible readings and activities.

Use the same questions as last week or choose new ones from the list. Give time for review of responses in the participant's workbook before the discussion begins. Write the questions you'll be using on a board or flip chart. Once again, encourage group members to listen for God in the responses of others in their small group.

Exploring the Word (20 minutes)

This exercise builds on the entry point for Romans 7:15, 21-25; 8:1-2.

Make a copy of the following reflection for each group member. Give each participant a copy and ask them to read noting words, phrases, or ideas that stand out.

> We tend to think of Jesus as the catalyst for change in individuals. We see believers in before-and-after pictures. Before Jesus: Sinner. After Jesus: Saved. Before-and-after pictures don't reflect the reality of the situation. Both before and after Jesus, we are sinners. We may try to do what is right. We may ask ourselves, What would Jesus do? But if we're honest, we know that we're sinners.
>
> The apostle Paul, who wrote the letter to the Romans, also saw Jesus as a catalyst for change. In Christ, God makes all things new. Paul talks about the world governed by sin and death and the world governed by the law of God, the old age and the new, life in the flesh and in the Spirit. All of these refer to the change God wants for the world. The before picture is a world defined by greed, individualism, power, ambition, self-absorption, oppression, illness, and poverty. God's new world is a picture of love, peace, health, well-being, grace, generosity, equality, justice, righteousness, long life, and full bellies.
>
> Paul understood that God's new world had not yet been established. We live in between. We see the after picture, and we believe that someday God's promises will be fulfilled. At the same time we live in the world, which looks a lot more like the before picture. Paul talks about struggling to do what is right, reaching for a world governed by God's grace. But every time he tries to do what is right, he gets caught up in the world governed by sin and death. So do we.
>
> Where does Jesus fit in? In Christ, the promises of God are sure. He preaches good

news to the poor, healing for the sick, freedom for the oppressed. He is, in himself, the presence of God in the world. Although we struggle with sin and fail to do what is right, we can rejoice in Christ because in him, we know what's coming. God's future, the establishment of a new creation on earth, is a sure thing.

Invite time for volunteers to share their reflections.

Then say, **We all experience an inner dialogue similar to the one Paul describes in Romans. What are those issues or times when you do what you don't want to do or do the very thing you hate?**

Take time to write out that inner dialogue much like Paul has done. You may even want to write it in a circle or long winding sentences to represent your thought patterns. When you have finished, pray that God would a provide a way to rescue you from this wretchedness. Share your reflections in groups of three.

Engaging the Word (lectio divina, 45 minutes)

Use the steps outlined for leading group *lectio* to guide the group through contemplation of **John 15:1-11**.

Closing (5 minutes)

Close your time together by asking participants what insights they have gained during the session. How has the scripture affected their relationship with God?

Sing a hymn, song, or chorus celebrating God's new creation. "This Is a Day of New Beginnings" and "Love Divine, All Loves Excelling" are good choices.

Invite the group to say together the Lord's Prayer.

Preparing for Session 7

- Complete the daily readings and entry-point responses in the participant's workbook.

- Read the introductions to Galatians, Ephesians, Philippians, and Colossians, First and Second Thessalonians, First and Second Timothy, Titus, and Philemon.

- Write and post the questions you will focus on in Interacting with the Word.

- Review the process for leading *lectio divina* until you feel comfortable using it, and photocopy and mark the passage for the alternate reader.

- Prepare materials for the worship center.

- Have available a CD player and a CD of Handel's *Messiah*; make copies of the words of the "Hallelujah" chorus.

- Cover a wall or table with several layers of paper. Have available paints, brushes, and paint shirts or smocks.

- Print closing responsive reading on newsprint.

Unity in

Christ

NOTE: All meeting outlines are for 90-minute sessions; if you are using this study in a 45-minute session, you will need to omit the *lectio divina* experience.

Opening (5 minutes)

Light the candle. Tell the group that you do so as a reminder of God's presence in the world and in our lives.

Propose that the group members consider one or two words describing the risen Christ as the group sings together the opening verses of a hymn, song, or chorus, such as "Jesus Shall Reign" or "Alleluia, Alleluia," in praise of the risen Christ.

Encourage volunteers to say their words aloud.

Sing together the closing verses of the chosen hymn.

Interacting with the Word (15 minutes)

Form small groups of three people to discuss the week's Bible readings and activities.

Use the same questions as last week, or choose new ones from the list. Give time for review of responses in the participant's workbook before the discussion begins. Write the questions you'll be using on a board or flip chart. Once again, encourage group members to listen for God in the responses of others in their small group.

Exploring the Word (20 minutes)

This activity builds on the entry point for Colossians 1:15-20.

Play the "Hallelujah" chorus from Handel's *Messiah*. Distribute words so that people can sing along if they choose.

Invite volunteers to read Colossians 1:15-20 aloud, each person reading a verse.

Say, **Colossians 1:15-20 is, first of all, a celebration of Christ's supremacy over all creation. "The kingdom of this world is become the kingdom of our Lord."**

Some Bibles title this passage of scripture "The Supremacy of Christ." Lead a discussion using the following questions. Encourage each member of the class to offer thoughts or reflections.
- What images in this passage represent Christ's supremacy?
- What does the passage mean by *supremacy*?
- How is Christ's supremacy similar to or different from the rulers of this world?

Take time to read this passage again on your own. In your journal answer the questions, "How do I experience Christ as supreme in my life? Where do I desire his supremacy in my life? in the world?" Allow time for journaling.

Provide paints and brushes. Give each person a paint shirt or smock. Cover a table or wall with several thicknesses of paper. Invite the participants to paint their response to the scripture, while listening to the "Hallelujah" chorus.

Engaging the Word (lectio divina, 45 minutes)

Use the steps outlined for leading group *lectio* to guide the group through contemplation of **Philippians 2:1-11**.

Closing (5 minutes)

Close your time together by asking participants what insights they gained during the session. How did the scripture deepen or change their relationship with God?

Sing a hymn, song, or chorus in praise of the risen Christ or play the "Hallelujah" chorus.

Invite the group to say responsively:
Jesus Christ is king of all creation.
> **Hallelujah!**

Jesus Christ is Lord of heaven and earth.
> **Hallelujah!**

In Jesus Christ, God has reconciled all of creation.
> **Hallelujah! Amen.**

Preparing for Session 8

- Complete the daily readings and entry-point responses in the participant's workbook.

- Read the introductions to Hebrews, James, First and Second Peter, Jude, and Revelation.

- Write and post the questions you will focus on in Interacting with the Word.

- Review the process for leading *lectio divina* until you feel comfortable using it, and photocopy and mark the passage for the alternate reader.

- Prepare materials for the worship center.

- Make a copy of the prayer quotations (page 54) for each participant; provide crayons, colored pencils, and blank paper.

- Print the closing statement on newsprint.

Faith in

Community

NOTE: All meeting outlines are for a 90-minute sessions; if you are using this study in a 45-minute session, you will need to omit the *lectio divina* experience.

Opening (5 minutes)

Light the candle. Tell the group that you do so as a reminder of God's presence in the world and in our lives.

Suggest that the members think about one or two words about prayer as the group sings the opening verses of a hymn, song, or chorus of prayer such as "Blest Be the Tie That Binds."

Invite participants to say their words aloud.

Sing the closing verses of the chosen hymn.

Interacting with the Word (15 minutes)

Invite participants to form small groups of three to discuss the week's Bible readings and activities.

Use the same questions as last week or choose new ones from the list. Give time for review of responses in the participant's workbook before the discussion begins. Write the questions you'll be using on a board or flip chart. Once again, encourage group members to listen for God in the responses of others in their small group.

Exploring the Word (20 minutes)

This activity builds on the entry point for James 5:13-20.

Give each participant a copy of the prayer quotations sheet found on page 54. Place crayons and colored pencils where all can access them.

Invite people to read and reflect on the quotations. Encourage them to write their responses on the front of the handout or in their journals.

After giving them enough time to read and silently respond, say:

As churches take on capital campaigns and dream of bigger buildings, up-to-date facilities, and more Sunday school classes, James reminds us that prayer builds a church. Each of the walls is only as strong as the prayer that discerned, envisioned, and consecrated them.

Take time now to draw on the back of the handout the walls of your church; draw them simply or elaborately. Then re-read the scripture, noting on your drawing those places where you have been comforted in your suffering, sung songs of praise, prayed for the sick, known God's forgiveness, or welcomed a new member into the body of Christ.

When everyone has had a chance to write and reflect, ask volunteers to show their drawings or describe moments of prayer and community that have been especially meaningful. Be aware that some may not be able to name occasions like these in their church but can name beautiful moments of grace and discipleship outside the church. Some persons may share painful experiences of shame or exclusion that happened within the walls of the church.

Next ask everyone to accompany you in a silent prayer walk through the halls of your church, praying that this would be a safe place, bathed in prayer, where people will meet God through Christ, and leave empowered by the Holy Spirit. Lead them through the foyer or gathering place, the worship space, the fellowship hall, the children's Sunday school rooms, and the youth area, the music room, and the pastor(s)' office. Return to your gathering place and ask each person for a brief reflection on this exercise.

NOTE: If you do not usually meet at the church, make a special effort to do so this week. If that is not possible, invite persons to move their fingers along the drawings they have created, silently praying for the church, as described above.

Engaging the Word (lectio divina, 45 minutes)

Use the steps outlined for leading group *lectio* to guide the group through contemplation of **Hebrews 13:1-6.**

Closing (5 minutes)

Close your time together by asking participants what insights they gained during the session. How did the scripture deepen or change their relationship with God?

Sing a hymn, song, or chorus praising God.

Invite the group to read in unison the prayer of the multitude in Revelation 19:6:

> Hallelujah!
> For the Lord our God
>   the Almighty reigns.

Thoughts on Prayer

Often prayer begins as a longing in the heart, a longing for love, . . . a longing to make contact with a Power greater than ourselves.
—Mark Yaconelli and Alexx Campbell, "Prayer," in *Way to Live: Christian Practices for Teens,* ed. Dorothy C. Bass and Don C. Richter (Nashville, TN: Upper Room Books, 2002), 278.

Pray as you can, not as you can't.
—Dom John Chapman, cited in Thelma Hall, *Too Deep for Words: Rediscovering Lectio Divina* (New York: Paulist Press, 1988), 40.

Whenever we pray, we pray with the whole people of God.
—Roberta C. Bondi, "The Paradox of Prayer," *Weavings: A Journal of the Christian Spiritual Life* (Mar/Apr 1989): 9.

Whatsoever we beg of God, let us also work for it.
—Jeremy Taylor

Our relationships with others flow directly from our primal way of being, which for the Christian is prayer.
—W. Paul Jones, "Prayer as Living itself," *Weavings: A Journal of the Christian Spiritual Life* (May/June 1998): 32

Prayer is by nature a dialog and a union with God. Its effect is to hold the world together. It achieves a reconciliation with God.
—Saint John Climacus (from http://www.stjrussianorthodox.com/prayers.htm)

Prayer stumbles over modern self-consciousness and self-reliance, a remarkably ingenuous belief in our ability to set goals and attain them as quickly as possible. . . . No wonder we have difficulty with prayer, for which the best how-to I know is from Psalm 46: "be still and know that I am God" . . . This can happen in an instant; it can also constitute a life's work.
—Kathleen Norris, *Amazing Grace: A Vocabulary of Faith* (New York: Riverhead Books, 1998), 61.

Permission is granted to make one copy for each participant.

Books of the

New Testament

Promises That Come True

Matthew writes this Gospel in the early church period when the church is predominantly Jewish. *Matthew frequently cites passages from the Old Testament that are fulfilled in the coming of Jesus the Messiah*, a watershed event in the long tradition of ancient Judaism. Matthew's intent is that those who read his Gospel, whether Jews or Gentiles, will see themselves as participants in the grand sweep of God's purposes in history. The coming of Jesus, says Matthew, is the culmination of all our waiting.

Matthew almost seems astonished *that God should become incarnate in Jesus Christ,* that people could see and hear and touch the Almighty God. As you read Matthew's Gospel, try to imagine yourself as a Jew in Gospel times. Your people have waited a thousand years for fulfillment. You have studied and remembered all the ancient prophecies and now, for the first time, they make sense. Suddenly, Almighty God is among your people. Emmanuel, *God is with us*, is present and active in the day-to-day life of the people—healing, feeding, teaching—bringing the word of God personally to the people of God.

As you read this Gospel, remember that *Jesus is still God with us*. He is God incarnate, with us in the Holy Spirit. What questions would you like to ask him? What would you like him to explain? What do you need him to do for you? What can you do for him? Make these questions the prayers of your heart.

> **Key Verse:** "Do not think that I have come to abolish the law or the prophets; I have come not to abolish but to fulfill." —Matthew 5:17

What It Costs to Follow Jesus

What did it cost Jesus to do the work of his Father? ***What will it cost you to follow Jesus?*** You will find the answers to both questions in the Gospel of Mark. In this fast-paced narrative, the writer reveals what it cost Jesus to do this work: He was persecuted by the Pharisees (Mark 3:6); he had to address the bewilderment expressed by his family (3:21); he was rejected by his hometown crowd (6:3-4); he relinquished both his privacy (6:30-34) and material goods. When accused, he did not defend himself (14:61).

Mark also outlines the cost of following Jesus. As much as we prefer to identify ourselves with Jesus in his role of conquering king, ***we are also called to become like him as servants, reconciling those around us to God.*** Just as Jesus spoke the truth to the confused and the corrupt, so must we. Just as he addressed the physical needs of the crowds who followed him, so must we. Just as he sought to heal the broken places of people's hearts, so must we.

As you read this account, let the forward momentum of Mark's narrative instill within you a sense of urgency. ***The time to follow Jesus is now.*** As you read about Jesus' words and works, ask God what he is calling you to be and do. What do you need to know about the power of Jesus and the servant heart of Jesus in order to be conformed to his image for the sake of others?

Key Verse: "For the Son of Man came not to be served but to serve, and to give his life a ransom for many." —Mark 10:45

Life of Prayer, Life of Compassion

The Gospel of Luke *draws a portrait of Jesus the Savior, who brings the love of God to earth and draws the people of God to heaven.* Luke conveys a fascination with this Jesus, a man of both prayer and action, who could be continually mindful of God and yet be fully present with people as an attentive, empathetic healer. Jesus modeled perfect communication with his heavenly Father (the Lord's Prayer) and perfect compassion for those his culture considered outcasts (the parable of the good Samaritan).

Jesus' life and teachings reconcile some of the contrasts that exist within the spiritual life, blending spiritual with physical (6:24-27), feasting with fasting (5:33-35), compassion with confrontation (6:9), and solitude with community (6:12-16).

Jesus moved beyond the restrictions of Jewish society, welcoming anyone with a seeking heart and granting the forgiveness of God to those the "righteous" Jewish leaders had rejected (6:20-26; 21:1-4). He engaged women, as well as men, in ministry (8:1-3; 23:55–24:11). For the only Gentile Gospel writer, this was good news indeed, for Jesus brought reconciliation to the Gentile world.

Let the book of Luke help you *discover what it means to live an inward life of prayer and an outward life of compassion.* When you struggle to balance "doing" with "being," imitate Jesus Christ who practiced an ongoing rhythm of ministry and sabbath rest. How can you serve God in the same radical way? How can you maintain this rhythm in your personal life?

Key Verses: "Lord, teach us to pray." —Luke 11:1

"Which of these . . . was a neighbor? . . . Go and do likewise." —Luke 10:36-37

Living in the Light

The light is shining. It is a light that defies our ability to capture and define. *The light has a voice that speaks life to us.* The light has hands that hold and heal us. The light has a name—Jesus, the son of Mary, the Son of God.

The light became flesh. The light conquers darkness and turns death into life. Into situations as ordinary as a catering problem at a wedding or as deeply troubling as a death in the family, this light beams a transforming power. *When the light is present, everything is changed.* When the light is present in us, we are changed. We have eternal life. We are restored to the glory that our Creator God intended.

Many situations in the book of John may resemble your personal situations. As you read you might ask yourself, *"What is God doing here, and how can I be open to allow God to work within me?"* As you participate in a community of believers, you might ask, "What is God doing among us?"

The Gospel writer calls his community of Jews and non-Jews to follow the revolutionary—and sometimes unpopular—way of Jesus. *He shows that the way of Jesus is full of challenge and adventure*—full of the risk involved when we let go and trust. The way might be hard. But in Jesus we find grace and truth. In Jesus we will "have life, and have it abundantly!" (John 10:10). The writer urges us to dwell in the light of Jesus, so that *we might carry the death-defying love of God into the world.*

Key Verse: The Word became flesh and lived among us, and we have seen his glory. . . . In him was life, and the life was the light of all people. —John 1:14, 4

The Good News Spreads under the Spirit's Guidance

This book might well be called "The Acts of the Holy Spirit." *From beginning to end the Spirit guides the spread of the gospel from Jerusalem to Rome itself.* Poured out on the day of Pentecost with "a sound like the rush of a violent wind" and "divided tongues, as of fire" (Acts 2:2-3), *the Spirit changes lives, alters plans, and transforms situations.* The Spirit empowers the early Christians to stand up to authorities, to face down mobs, to speak to hostile audiences, and to hold fast through suffering even to death—all for the sake of the good news of Jesus Christ. At the same time, the Spirit impels them far beyond their comfort zones into missions to the Samaritans and Gentiles and to people from all levels of society.

God's Spirit is active in our own lives—comforting, encouraging, strengthening, nudging. When have you felt led, like the early disciples, in a particular direction? When have you been the channel of God's love to someone else? When have you experienced a shower of grace when you needed it most? And when have you found resources of strength to do what seemed impossible? *You have experienced the work of the Spirit*, sent by Jesus Christ who "is exalted at the right hand of God, and [who has] received from the Father the promise of the Holy Spirit, . . . [and] has poured out this that you both see and hear" (2:33).

Key Verse: "But you will receive power when the Holy Spirit has come upon you; and you will be my witnesses in Jerusalem, in all Judea and Samaria, and to the ends of the earth." —Acts 1:8

The Old Self and the New Self

Like a parent giving a gift to a child out of pure love, **God gives us the gift of salvation.** We do not have to do anything to deserve it, and we never could be good enough to earn it. In the book of Romans, the apostle Paul writes a treatise on the love of God. God's love is redeeming love, for every one of us is "under the power of sin" (3:9) and controlled by our human nature; we all "fall short of the glory of God" (3:23). **God initiates our redemption even before we are aware of our need of it.** In response to God's love, we are to turn our entire lives toward God so that, day by day, we are transformed—a process (5:1-4) that involves heart (2:29), mind (8:5-6), will (7:14-15), and actions (12:9-21)—as we become new persons who want what God wants (12:2).

Romans is a theological book, but it is also a realistic, practical discussion of how growing into fullness of life in Christ is a matter of mind, heart, and spirit. Throughout our inner struggles and our struggles with others, we are drawn by God's incredible love in Christ Jesus, which seeks us out and bears us along in the spiritual life. Nothing that we have done, or ever could do, can separate us from the love that God offers us in Christ Jesus our Lord.

> ***Key Verse:*** But God proves his love for us in that while we still were sinners Christ died for us.
> —Romans 5:8

The Way of Love

In the apostle Paul's first letter to the Corinthians we encounter a missionary whose spirit is being transformed by the Holy Spirit. *Paul urges the people of the Corinthian church to be likewise transformed by the Spirit of God.* Paul admits that he is not a clever, eloquent orator but a childlike man who is "foolish" enough to preach the cross (1:17–2:16). *His servant posture cuts through the barriers of human factions to pull together a community of believers* who will proclaim in one voice that Jesus is Lord.

As you read Paul's letter and meditate on it, *imagine yourself in the presence of the apostle, a seasoned spiritual teacher who crowns his letter with the often-quoted essay on love.* Envision yourself telling Paul how hard it is for you to uphold this standard of love when you've had a spat with your spouse or felt misunderstood by your friend. Then turn your thoughts toward God in prayer. Ask God to help you cross the bridge between love in the abstract ("Of course I love people, but I can't stand my next-door neighbor!") and love in the concrete ("I know if I can learn to love my neighbor, then it won't be so hard to love other people"). *How might such prayerful interaction with what Paul writes help you to become more loving—and part of a more loving community in Jesus Christ?*

Key Verse: Love is patient; love is kind; love is not envious or boastful or arrogant or rude. It does not insist on its own way; it is not irritable or resentful; it does not rejoice in wrongdoing, but rejoices in the truth. It bears all things, believes all things, hopes all things, endures all things.
—1 Corinthians 13:4-7

Second Corinthians

Our Hope for New Life

***One of the greatest obstacles facing us on the road to spiritual formation is
our lack of appreciation for our infinite worth in the eyes of God.*** No
matter what faults and failings may hamper us on our way home to
our Father's house, God loves and forgives and welcomes us. ***One of
the gifts the apostle Paul gives his readers in this ardent and honest letter is
a renewed sense of worthiness to minister in the name of Jesus Christ.*** Paul
applies correction but he also encourages his readers with an
appraisal of their worth: They are "the aroma of Christ" (2:15);
Christ's "ambassadors" (5:20); "the temple of the living God" (6:16).
Paul's encouragement is not meant to produce pride in his readers
but to remind them that "Jesus Christ is in [them]" (13:5). His spirit
forms, reforms, and transforms us "into the same image from one
degree of glory to another" (3:18).

The spirit of servanthood dies, as Paul sees it, when we try to become
"super-apostles" (12:11), incapable of admitting that we are
vulnerable, suffering, wounded creatures. ***We can unlock the door
to Christian service only with the key of our weaknesses.*** Paul boasts of his
"weaknesses, so that the power of Christ may dwell in [him]" (12:9).

As you read this letter, reflect on your ministry, whatever it may be.
What do you think makes you competent to serve? ***What are your
strengths in Christ Jesus?*** How are his strengths apparent through
your weaknesses?

Key Verse: So if anyone is in Christ, there is a new creation: everything old has passed away; see,
everything has become new! All this is from God, who reconciled us to himself through Christ, and
has given us the ministry of reconciliation; that is, in Christ God was reconciling the world to himself, not counting their trespasses against them. —2 Corinthians 5:17-19

In Step with the Spirit

Parades are fun to watch, but it takes great concentration to march in one, especially if one is playing an instrument or carrying a flag. Bands designate a leader to set the proper cadence; the challenge for each band member is to stay in step—and not only when the band is in front of the viewing stand!

Paul's letter to the Galatians explores some of the difficulties that can cause Christians to get out of step as they follow Jesus Christ. Paul warns his readers against misunderstanding the role of the law, pursuing the dead end of human effort, and concentrating on external religious practice while neglecting their inner life.

Paul's letter is a refreshing message for the Galatians—and for us today: we don't have to struggle to be in control of our spiritual life. *God wants to guide us as we walk in step with the Holy Spirit so that we experience God's gracious freedom, guidance, and renewing joy.* As you read this letter, consider how your own lifestyle reflects the pace and power of the Holy Spirit. Be careful to notice those areas in which *God is calling you to get in step with the Spirit.*

> *Key Verse:* If we live by the Spirit, let us also be guided by the Spirit. —Galatians 5:25

Rooted in Love

This letter to the Ephesians reminds us of the importance of roots. The health of a tree is dependent on the health of its root system. Roots reach deep into the soil to draw up the necessary nourishment to sustain the tree. Deep roots create stability and help the tree withstand the storms of life. Likewise, *when we are rooted in the powerful and boundless love of Jesus, we are prepared to face the challenges of living in a stormy world.*

This letter calls us to imitate God (5:1) as the means of developing healthy roots. That task is made possible by being in a community of love with other Christians (4:12-16). Furthermore, *our life is energized by the unconditional grace of Jesus rather than by our own human efforts (2:4-10).* Throughout this letter Paul (the attributed writer) offers prayers for his readers.

Pay attention to your own root system as you read and pray through Ephesians. *Pray that Jesus Christ will dwell within your heart more and more so that you are equipped to face the realities of life.* Consider the spiritual habits that have sustained you in the past. What new resources does this book offer to you? *How can you encourage others in the healthy planting of their roots deep into Jesus?*

Key Verse: I pray . . . that Christ may dwell in your hearts through faith, as you are being rooted and grounded in love. I pray that you may have the power to comprehend, with all the saints, what is the breadth and length and height and depth, and to know the love of Christ that surpasses knowledge. —Ephesians 3:16-19

 *Philippians*

A Work in Progress

One of the characteristics of our contemporary culture is impatience. *Advances in technology encourage us to demand ever more in less time.* Unfortunately the continued pressure to rush everything has reduced our ability to wait for anything.

Some aspects of life, however, cannot be rushed. *Spiritual growth is no different than physical growth—both require time and great patience.* And when we experience growth, it is not always easy to detect. Progress sometimes seems meager. Perhaps that is why Christians have often been called a pilgrim people. *Our lives reflect the process of God's work more than any polished final product.*

In an age of instant gratification, the apostle *Paul proclaims a countercultural message.* He reminds us to be patient because God's work in us is not finished. Regardless of how long we have been concentrating on growing spiritually, *we are still beginners—and always will be*—until we reach heaven. Paul encourages us to press on and not give up. He emphasizes that *Christian maturity is a process of cooperating with God's presence and power in our lives.*

The message of Philippians is one of patience and hope. *Perhaps this book will renew your stagnant life or give you permission to seek excellence rather than perfection in all you do.* Regardless of where you find yourself, let these words inspire and invite you into deeper participation with the God who seeks to join you in spiritual partnership.

> ***Key Verse:*** I am confident of this, that the one who began a good work among you will bring it to completion by the day of Jesus Christ. —Philippians 1:6

A Heart Set on God

Sometimes we fool ourselves, believing it is more difficult to live today than two thousand years ago. However the Christians of the first century faced equal or greater challenges to their faith. *The writer seeks to etch deeply into human hearts the truth that meaning and purpose do not come through any exclusive knowledge or superior spirituality.* Rather they are firmly established in the life of Jesus Christ, in whom God was pleased to dwell with all the divine fullness. Paul (the attributed writer) understands the serious crisis before his readers and seeks to weave these words into a fabric of practical guidance that clothes them with hearts that seek to focus on God. *In pondering these words of scripture, remember that the Bible uses the word "heart" to speak of mind, soul, and will.* How can the book of Colossians help you devote your life to God in all of these areas?

Key Verse: So if you have been raised with Christ, seek the things that are above, where Christ is, seated at the right hand of God. —Colossians 3:1

First Thessalonians

Waiting in Holiness

How often we wish for a friend who could give us spiritual help—not just casual advice but powerful counsel that would lead us to a closer relationship with God (2:12). The Christians of Thessalonica had such a friend in the apostle Paul. As he writes, ***Paul is open about his affection for them, his longing to be their guide and religious instructor, and his pride in their success in living lives worthy of God's calling.*** He is thrilled when Timothy reports that the faith and love Paul remembered as characteristic of them was still alive and flourishing among these faithful converts.

Paul's affection for the Thessalonians is so endearing that we might be reminded of a similar friend of our own. ***Imagine returning home one day and finding a letter waiting in the mail from just such an old friend.*** More than once you have wished you could sit and talk with this friend because he or she is a good listener and always knows just what to say to point you in the right direction.

Now imagine that this friend is someone like Paul, a person of considerable stature, who is keenly interested in the things you do, say, and think. In your last letter to this friend, what did you write about? What was weighing heavily on your heart? What joys did you share? Now how does this person's letter of response to you begin? ***What concern seems most important?*** What does your friend wish for you most of all? Read the book of First Thessalonians as if it were such a letter, written just for you and your faith community.

> ***Key Verse:*** And may he so strengthen your hearts in holiness that you may be blameless before our God and Father at the coming of our Lord Jesus with all his saints. —1 Thessalonians 3:13

A Life Worthy of God's Calling

The early church in Thessalonica is buzzing with predictions of Jesus' second coming. For some the fearful "end times" are troubling to contemplate. Others want only to wait passively for Jesus' return. The timing of this final event is uncertain, and many, in a state of paralysis, have given up their work and sit idly, awaiting the end of the world.

The author of this letter pointedly reminds his readers of who is in charge of all these things. The apostle Paul (the attributed writer) admonishes the Thessalonians not to be shaken but to have faith (2:2), remembering that God has chosen them.

Paul also confronts the destructiveness of fear and anxiety. They are to remain steadfast in their faith in the same way God is steadfast in God's love for them (2:15-16). Idleness only adds to the problem of worry, he says; and *he tells them to earn their own way (3:11-12) and live their lives as models of love and perseverance (3:5).*

Take time to reflect on your fears as you read Second Thessalonians. Which fears can you surrender to God? *How could a fuller measure of faith in God dispel your feelings of being overwhelmed and hopeless in your daily life?* What do you need to allow God to handle so that you can experience a turnabout in your ability to handle your fears? As you read this letter, *let yourself experience the presence of the One who can calm all your fears.*

Key Verse: To this end we always pray for you, asking that our God will make you worthy of his call and will fulfill by his power every good resolve and work of faith. —2 Thessalonians 1:11

Guidelines for Godliness

As the young pastor Timothy's mentor and friend, the apostle Paul (the attributed writer) writes to his "loyal child in the faith" with words of instruction and encouragement. *Timothy is pastoring a church that faces all the problems of a growing institution, not the least of which is keeping the church's love for Jesus Christ fresh and fervent (see Revelation 2:4).* Timothy has to manage the church's internal affairs such as personnel, structure, worship, and doctrinal struggles as well as to combat the continuing persecution and false teachings coming from outside and inside the church.

The book of First Timothy is primarily a call to godliness in the broadest sense. *Paul summons the congregation to godliness characterized by right doctrine, orderly worship, and holy relationships.* He addresses the mission of the church, the qualifications of leaders, and social concerns such as the care of widows.

To be godly is to imitate God in holiness; such a calling affects every part of our being, from our beliefs to our behavior, from our attitudes to our actions, and from our relationships to our worship. There isn't an element of human existence that isn't radically and profoundly altered by this call to Christian living that Paul refers to as godliness. Consider studying this book with a sheet of paper with the word *godliness* written at the top. Ask God to broaden your view of godliness and to remove the limits of your previous definition of the word. *Ask God to show you areas of your life that need to be anointed with new holiness.*

Key Verse: Pay close attention to yourself and to your teaching; continue in these things, for in doing this you will save both yourself and your hearers. —1 Timothy 4:16

Second Timothy

Faithfulness under Pressure

Do you ever live through seasons in which the entire world seems bent on distracting you from God's calling? *As you seek to serve God, are you hampered by pressures and opposition?* If so, this letter will offer you profound encouragement. Whether your frustrations stem from the pressure of meeting many obligations, a feeling of weariness, or the experience of open opposition or ridicule, you will find empathy in Paul's and Timothy's experiences. Even as they face many of these same pressures, *Paul (the attributed writer) urges Timothy to persevere and remain faithful in his ministry.*

While most of the New Testament books are written to churches, this one is written to an individual. The situation in which Paul and Timothy find themselves is a veritable pressure cooker. Paul is in prison; the church is being persecuted; opposition is hot and fierce— even from those who call themselves Christians, and *Timothy is trying to stay true to his work in the midst of doctrinal confusion and hardship. Paul's letter is a stirring call to Timothy to remain faithful under pressure*, and its relevance has been proven in every generation.

Before you reflect on the specific teachings of this book, take a personal inventory of the challenges you have faced in serving God. *What has made it most difficult for you to fulfill a calling that you believe God has given you?* What is the biggest obstacle you currently face? Even as you confront your own struggles, prepare to be challenged and encouraged by Paul's words to his friend Timothy. Within these chapters you may find the keys to remaining faithful under pressure in your own life.

> *Key Verse:* As for you, always be sober, endure suffering, do the work of an evangelist, carry out your ministry fully. —2 Timothy 4:5

Keeping Your Focus

Have you ever heard of the phrase "medical triage"? It refers to the practice of responding to natural or human disasters. ***When the injured are so many and the physicians are so few, doctors and nurses must set priorities and work systematically***; otherwise they'd be overwhelmed and the situation would take much longer to bring under control.

On a spiritual level, this was the challenge Titus faced. He is left on the Mediterranean island of Crete to supervise a church planted among a particularly unruly people. The people of Crete were renowned for their malicious savagery and unrestrained passions. The idiom "to play the Cretan" meant to be a liar. Even Epimenides, one of Crete's own philosophers, chastised his homeland's moral character. These are the issues the writer takes up with Titus. By giving concrete advice in a clear framework, he seems to be saying, ***"Don't be overwhelmed; stay focused; appoint qualified elders; challenge false teaching; pass on pure doctrine; and don't forget the importance of good deeds."***

This letter encapsulates the heart of true Christianity. Titus is overwhelmed, so the writer focuses only on what was most important. The challenge Titus faced long ago can result in something good for us today, for in this letter we are presented with the bedrock essence of our faith. ***If you were left alone on an island to nurture a Christian church that had been planted in this culture, what would you emphasize?*** How would you bring order? What would be your primary message?

Key Verse: I left you behind in Crete for this reason, so that you should put in order what remained to be done, and should appoint elders in every town, as I directed you. —Titus 1:5

Philemon

A Plea for Reconciliation

This brief letter leads us into the middle of a difficult situation in the early church, one with parallels to our time. *Philemon was a first-century Christian living in Asia Minor.* His slave Onesimus escaped and met the imprisoned apostle Paul, who shared the gospel with him. Then Paul wrote this gracious and respectful letter encouraging Philemon to take back Onesimus—"no longer as a slave but . . . [as] a beloved brother" (v. 16).

Consider Philemon's options. *Should he free Onesimus and risk total chaos among the other slaves, who might fake conversions to win their freedom?* Should he punish Onesimus for running away? Should he return Onesimus to Paul? Or should he do what Paul suggests—welcome him home as a brother in Christ Jesus?

Welcoming people into our church communities after they have a change of heart can be a problem for us. If they have hurt us in the past, we may want to offer only the cold heart and closed fist of judgment. We may feel little eagerness to remove the stigma associated with their former reputations. After all, what will everyone else think if it looks like we are too easy on them?

But Paul takes a different approach by regarding other Christians as family members. Philemon is twice addressed as "brother." Apphia is a "sister." Because Onesimus is now a Christian, he too must be called "brother." *The apostle Paul encourages Philemon to do the hard thing— the right thing.* His letter asks us to do the same in the difficult relationships we may face in our own churches.

Key Verse: So if you consider me your partner, welcome him as you would welcome me.
—Philemon 17

A New and Better Way

Some people think that, in religious matters, tradition is all-important. Some, on the other hand, will have nothing to do with tradition; they forever want to be on the "cutting edge." Ideally, though, *the best of the new is that which grows from and builds on the depth and wisdom of the older traditions.*

For the writer of Hebrews, *the new covenant of Jesus Christ represented the fullness and completion of the revelation of God's love for humanity—the revelation God began with the old covenant.* In fact the Old Testament itself pointed to the unfolding of the new covenant of love in Jesus Christ—a new and superior way that would supersede the old.

As you read and meditate on these pages of scripture, notice how often they refer to Jesus' ministry as "superior to" or "better" than the ministry of the old covenant. *This book is about faith—God's faithfulness to us in giving us his Son, "the reflection of God's glory and the exact imprint of God's very being" (1:3),* and our faithful response to "looking to Jesus" (12:2). Open up any areas in your life in which you need to renew your trust and dependence on the promises of God and the provisions of Jesus Christ through the Holy Spirit.

Key Verse: For this reason he is the mediator of a new covenant, so that those who are called may receive the promised eternal inheritance, because a death has occurred that redeems them from the transgressions under the first covenant. —Hebrews 9:15

Faith at Work

James could be said to have one objective in writing this letter: *to assist the churches to whom he writes to live well, that is, to work out their faith in good deeds and holy habits.* The straightforward, commonsense approach of this letter is refreshing, although *it might challenge and confront those who are comfortable in certain patterns of neglect or indifference toward others.* "Be doers of the word, and not merely hearers who deceive themselves" (1:22). "Understand this" (1:19). "You do well if you really fulfill the royal law" (2:8). These are the directives of a writer who is intent on reiterating or fleshing out the ancient words of the prophet Micah: "He has told you, O mortal, what is good; and what does the LORD require of you but to do justice, and to love kindness, and to walk humbly with your God?" (6:8).

As you contemplate these chapters, *let them be like candles lighting your soul, life, and habits.* How do they describe you or your church? How do they challenge you toward greater faithfulness in loving others? In the down-to-brass-tacks spirit of this letter, consider this question throughout: *What are specific and concrete ways in which I can respond to what I am reading?* Ask God to lead you into authentic behaviors and attitudes that—in challenging ways and ways that may stretch you perhaps—will put your faith to work.

> **Key Verse:** But be doers of the word, and not merely hearers who deceive themselves.
> —James 1:22

First Peter

Christians under Construction

Standing fast in the true grace of God transforms all of life. How simple it sounds. How seldom it is achieved! Peter (the attributed writer) knows this from personal experience. He knows how easy it is to wobble and fall. With a pastor's heart of compassion, he writes to Christians scattered in many places and facing a variety of tests and trials. *His warm, encouraging letter reminds them first of the blessings and hope they already have in Jesus Christ.* With that confident assurance they have every reason to be diligent in putting aside anything that could hold them back from full enjoyment of salvation.

The Christian life is no glowing dream world though. Peter is realistic. *Believers are to hold on in the midst of political challenges, slavery, abuse, questions from unbelievers, and suffering and pain.* Standing fast in these situations requires a clear sense of God's gracious presence. It also demands a disciplined commitment to living daily according to Jesus' example. Peter gives down-to-earth, specific guidance. *This is Christianity in everyday clothes.*

Even outright persecution is not to shake Jesus' followers from standing fast. As painful and puzzling as it is to suffer because of their faith, Peter's readers can be encouraged because of his gentle reminder that they share in Christ's sufferings.

Peter shows the care of a wise shepherd in the way he writes to his readers. His letter encourages us to care for others in the same way. *Humbled, disciplined, and strengthened by the power of Jesus Christ, we can stand firm in the amazing, true grace of God.*

Key Verse: I have written this short letter to encourage you and to testify that this is the true grace of God. Stand fast in it. —1 Peter 5:12

Second Peter

Listening for Truth

Would you prefer a godly life or a wallow in the mud (2:22)? Given the choice, most Christians would choose a godly life! Peter (the attributed writer) dramatically contrasts those two choices. He asserts that *everything needed for living a godly life has already been given us in Christ Jesus; it is simply waiting to be appropriated.* If this is the case, who would ever be diverted? "Well," says Peter, "plenty of people!" He pulls no punches. The examples he uses do not make for pleasant reading. Yet, shock tactics have their place in demanding our attention.

These particular shock tactics provide the basis for Peter's heartfelt exhortation that his readers be on the lookout for similar issues that might undermine their faith. *God is patient and leaves time for each generation of believers to identify the options and choose salvation and life.* But one day time will run out. How much better to be actively involved in growing in grace than to be caught unprepared.

The message of this letter is quite contemporary. Nothing has changed—God provides everything we need for a life of godliness. *We face the same challenge the early Christians did—to grow in our knowledge and experience of holiness in Jesus Christ.* Nothing has changed, either, in the human capacity to distort, scoff at, or simply disbelieve the grace of God. We, like the recipients of Peter's letter, have been forewarned: stay away from the mud and discover the green pastures of godliness!

> *Key Verse:* Grow in the grace and knowledge of our Lord and Savior Jesus Christ. —2 Peter 3:18

Living in Love

John's letter paints a panoramic portrait of love the way God sees it. As we read and pray through these brief but powerful pages, two facets of biblical love seem to stand out. First, *before we are able to practice or walk in love, we must have some awareness of its nature.* Love is grounded in God (4:8, 16) and is most clearly depicted in Jesus Christ, who sacrificially offered his life for us (3:16; 4:10). *John calls us to the same kind of sacrificial love in which our actions align with our words in truth (3:18).*

Second, the apostle John (the attributed writer) connects love with obedience. *Obedience is our joyful response to the love of Jesus Christ, which allows us to live in him and he in us* (2:3-5; 2 John 5-6). We are commanded to walk in love not only when it is convenient for us but each day because we are children of God (5:2).

As you reflect on these words, *review your experience of God's incredible love for you.* Think about how you express that love to others. And as you ponder this message, prayerfully *ask God to help you to see God more clearly, love God more dearly, and follow God more nearly* as you mirror divine love day by day.

Key Verse: God is love, and those who abide in love abide in God, and God abides in them.
—1 John 4:16

Walking in Love

Biblical love is contagious! *Love is a dynamic, blazing flame that awakens us by its power, passion, and reality.* However, our life experiences remind us that not everyone is inspired by the integrity of love. As strange as it may seem, some are equally motivated by error. This brief letter summarizes the battle being waged within the believer between walking in love and walking in error. *True love—expressed in obedience—produces the richness of delight in God (v. 6).* But walking in error and heresy yields the emptiness of deception and danger (vv. 7-11). John (the attributed writer) alerts us to the same potential pitfalls today. As you read this short book, don't underestimate the importance of its message. *Whom or what do you welcome into your life?* Do those people, activities, and experiences encourage you to walk in love or in error?

> ***Key Verse:*** This is the commandment just as you have heard it from the beginning—you must walk in it. —2 John 6

Walking in Truth

What a startling comparison John (the attributed writer) paints on the canvas of this book of holy scripture. *Two specific individuals are mentioned by name to illustrate the importance of personal character.* Diotrephes, who is characterized by self-love, exhibits an inhospitable attitude that ravages the Christian community (vv. 9-10). In stark contrast is Demetrius, whose reputation for truthful living is affirmed by everyone (v. 12). His life is marked by integrity, and John holds him up as a fitting model for his readers. It is evident from John's words that *walking in truth is more than speaking the correct words. It requires the formation of character that is honest and is worthy of God.* Indeed John's third letter could serve as a New Testament counterpoint to Micah's great ethical summary of the law: "He has told you, O mortal, what is good; and what does the LORD require of you but to do justice, and to love kindness, and to walk humbly with your God?" (6:8).

Key Verse: I have no greater joy than this, to hear that my children are walking in the truth.
—3 John 4

Standing Firm

This little book is short, sharp, and salutary. *Jude sets out to write an enthusiastic letter about the wonders of salvation but finds himself writing strong, stern words instead.* He is motivated by love of God and love for his readers.

Jude (the attributed writer, who is said by tradition to be the brother of Jesus as well as his servant) burns with passion for the purity of the faith; he can't bear to see it undermined. But that is exactly what is happening, and a warning must be issued. With anguish and energy Jude startles his readers into taking notice. At the beginning and end of the letter, Jude speaks of the mercy, peace, love, power, and security that are available in Jesus Christ. In the middle of the letter, Jude gives graphic examples of the awful possibility of perverting what Jesus offers. Though the examples Jude gives certainly would have evoked powerful memories for his original readers, some of them may seem irrelevant to us in our culture and our time. We can't escape the significance of this letter however. God's Spirit, who inspired Jude's letter, asks us to consider what might pervert God's grace in our day. *What behavior, lifestyle, attitudes, or destructive talk do we need to address?* Do we need to wake up? After all, we are nearer to the "last time" than Jude's readers were! May his passionate words kindle the fire of love in our hearts. Be warned. Take action. *Keep yourself in the love of God.*

Key Verse: Keep yourselves in the love of God; look forward to the mercy of our Lord Jesus Christ that leads to eternal life. —Jude 21

Revelation

A Kingdom of Priests

The book of Revelation paints sweeping landscapes of two worlds: the sinful world that will pass away ("'Fallen, fallen is Babylon the great!'" [18:2]) and, in contrast, a new world established in Jesus Christ that is the true home of all believers ("I saw the holy city, the new Jerusalem, coming down out of heaven from God" [21:2]).

There are many interpretations of this apocalyptic book. Some interpret it as exclusively futuristic and place the events of the book in the end times. This view, however, avoids the call to radical discipleship at the heart of John's vision. ***Revelation can be seen as a map of the Christian's spiritual journey from citizenship in Babylon to citizenship in the new Jerusalem.*** Babylon represents all the destructive, self-centered, dehumanizing effects of sin in this world, while Jerusalem represents the healing and liberation of new life in Christ. Redeemed in the blood of the Lamb of God, ***believers find a new identity in Jesus Christ and become "priests" of God*** who represent the presence of God in the fallen world.

As you meditate on John's vision, try to put aside all your preconceptions about Revelation and listen to the voice of the Spirit speaking to your heart about your true life as a "priest" in God's kingdom. ***Listen for God's call for you to become what you were created to be—a beloved child created in the image of God, a member of God's kingdom.*** Let the love of God become evident in you as you live in profound integrity and wholeness.

> ***Key Verse:*** To him who loves us and freed us from our sins by his blood, and made us to be a kingdom, priests serving his God and Father, to him be glory and dominion forever and ever. Amen.
> —Revelation 1:5-6

What Is

Spiritual Formation?

HUMAN BEINGS ARE creatures of the future. Unlike other inhabitants of creation whose lives are fixed within the boundaries of genetics and instinct, human existence is open-ended, laced with mystery, like moist clay in a potter's hand. We are works in progress, shaped by the constant rhythms of nature and the unexpected turns of history. Sometimes elated and sometimes burdened by our unfinished condition, we live our days conscious that "what we will be has not yet been made known" (1 John 3:2). A sense of our true identity is always just beyond our grasp, always awaiting us, it seems, just around the next bend in the road.

As nature and history interact with a human existence that is incomplete, pliable and rich with significant potential, personal formation occurs. ***Human beings are formed by the sculpting of will, intellect, and emotion into a distinct way of being in the world.*** Such formation of personal character will assume a wide range of expression depending on our location geographically, socially, economically and culturally. Family values, social conventions, cultural assumptions, the great turning points of an epoch, the painful secrets of a heart—these and many other factors combine to form or deform the direction, depth and boundaries of our lives. Formation is therefore a fundamental characteristic of human life. It is happening whether or not we are aware of it, and its effect may as often inhibit as promote the development of healthy, fulfilled humanity.

For people of biblical faith, nature and history of themselves are not the final sources of personal formation. Rather, they are means through which the God who formed all things molds human beings into the contours of their truest destiny: the unfettered praise of God (see Isaiah 43:21). To be shaped by God's gracious design is a particular expression of personal formation—spiritual formation. Irenaeus, third-century bishop of Lyons, echoed this ancient biblical theme when he observed that *"the glory of God is the human being fully alive."* The God known in scripture is a God who continuously forms something out of nothing—earth and heaven, creatures great and small, a people who call upon God's name, the "inmost being" (Psalm 139:13) of every human life. Yet the majestic sweep of God's formational activity never eclipses the intimacy God desires and seeks with us. Having carefully and lovingly formed each of us in the womb, God knows us by name and will not forget us (see Isaiah 43:1; 44:21, 24). In the biblical perspective, to be a person means to exist in a relationship of ongoing spiritual formation with the God whose interest in us extends to the very roots of our being.

For Christians, the pattern and fulfillment of God's work of spiritual formation converge in a single figure—Jesus Christ. Jesus is the human being fully alive, fully open to God's work in the world. Simultaneously, Jesus is God's work fully alive, fully embodied in the world. For all who are heavily burdened and wearied by the torments of the world, for all who long to dwell in the house of the Lord, Jesus is the level way, the whole truth and the radiant life. Christians are placed daily before the greatest of all choices: *to be conformed to the luminous image of Jesus Christ* through the gracious assistance of God the Holy Spirit or to be conformed to the ravaged image of the world through the deceitful encouragement of the "powers of this dark world" (Romans 12:2; Ephesians 6:10-13).

Spiritual formation in the Christian tradition, then, is a lifelong process through which our new humanity, hidden with Jesus Christ in God, becomes ever more visible and effective through the leading of the Holy Spirit. *Spiritual formation at its best has been understood to be at once fully divine and fully human—that is, initiated by God and manifest in both vital communities of faith and in the lives of individual disciples.* We see this theme carried through the history of the church, from Paul's introduction of formation in Jesus Christ as the central work of Christian life (Galatians 4:19) to early formational writings such as the Didache (second century); to the formative intent of monastic rules; to the shaping purpose of Protestant manuals of piety; to the affirmation of lay formation in the documents of Vatican II; and finally to the current search for practices that open us to God.

OUR NEW HUMANITY

Our unfinished character leads us to acknowledge that *"what we will be has not yet been made known."* Yet Christians, looking at Jesus Christ, can add with confident hope that "we shall be like him" (1 John 3:2). This hope originates in the hidden dimensions of baptism. Baptism unites us with the full sweep of Jesus' life and death, resurrection, and ascension in glory to the eternal communion of love enjoyed by our triune God. In baptism, motifs of cleansing from the stain of sin coexist with images of death and rebirth to signal the radically new life we enter through this spiritual birth canal (John 3:1-6).

At the center of this rebirth from above is the Paschal mystery—*the pattern of self-relinquishment and loving availability Jesus freely manifested in his ministry and in his final journey* to Jerusalem and Golgotha. This is the mysterious pattern of God's work in the world, the pattern of loss that brings gain, willing sacrifice that yields abundance, self-forgetfulness that creates a space for the remembering God. It is the pattern that steers our course from bondage to freedom—from the ways of the old Adam, who turned and hid from the One who so lovingly formed him, *to the freedom of the new Adam*, Jesus Christ, who lives with God in unbroken intimacy.

This unfolding of baptismal grace in daily life, this passing from bondage to freedom, is spiritual formation. Because *spiritual formation draws us into the fullness of life in Jesus Christ*, it shares the qualities of Jesus Christ. Thus, spiritual formation is eminently personal yet inherently corporate: *It erases nothing of our unique humanity but transposes it into a larger reality*—the mystical body of Jesus Christ in and through which we are, as the Episcopal Book of Common Prayer notes, "very members incorporate" of one another. Spiritual formation is also fully human, reflecting our own decisions, commitments, disciplines and actions. At the same time, *spiritual formation is wholly divine, an activity initiated by God and completed by God*, in which we have been generously embraced for the sake of the world.

THE HOLY SPIRIT'S LEADING

The sweeping movement of grace by which the world was created and is sustained is orchestrated by God the Holy Spirit. In God's sovereign freedom, the Holy Spirit stirs where the Spirit chooses. Remarkably, *the Spirit has selected human life as a privileged place of redemptive activity.* In the day-to-day rhythms of our life, the Holy Spirit comes to us with gentle persistence, inviting us to join the wondrous dance of life with God. In this holy dance the Spirit always takes the lead, a partner both sensitive and sure. ***"The spiritual life is the life of God's Spirit in us,"*** notes spiritual writer Marjorie Thompson, "the living interaction between our spirit and the Holy Spirit through which we mature into the full stature of Christ and become more surrendered to the work of the Spirit within and around us."

There are settings and disciplines that prepare us to recognize and respond to the Holy Spirit's invitation. The church, the body of Jesus Christ visible and tangible in the world, as rich with promise as it is with paradox—is the principal context in which to sharpen our spiritual senses. The mere fact of gathering with others on the Lord's Day reminds us that the Holy Spirit continuously draws together what evil strives to scatter. In congregational worship, we hear God's word to us; recall how lavishly God loves us; see this love enacted in baptism; taste its sweetness and its wonder in the Lord's Supper; and take stock of our response to it in confession, hymn and corporate prayer. Small groups given to prayer, study or outreach also offer places to increase our awareness of the Holy Spirit's leading. In the company of faithful seekers, another person's moment of vulnerability, a truth spoken in love or a story told in trust can awaken insight into ways the Holy Spirit is also present with us. Family life, which Martin Luther placed ahead of the monastery as the true school of charity, provides many opportunities to learn the art of self-forgetfulness. ***Time spent with the poor and needy instructs us in our own poverty,*** prepares us to receive more than we bestow from those who often seem so distressingly different and gives the Spirit occasion to teach us the extent of our common humanity.

Personal spiritual practices also prime us to be responsive to the Holy Spirit's approach. The meditative reading of scripture encouraged in this Bible enables us to become at home in God's word. As this occurs, we develop a growing familiarity with the Holy Spirit who fashioned and continues to dwell in holy writ. According to twelfth-century Cistercian abbot Peter of Celle, such reading is nothing less than "the soul's food, light, lamp, refuge, consolation, and the spice of every spiritual savor." ***Prayer, that royal road to deepening intimacy with God, will inevitably acquaint us with the guiding grace of the Spirit.*** It is in the Spirit that we pray and through the Spirit that the inarticulate yearnings of our heart receive coherent expression before God (see Romans 8:27). Various "spiritual fitness" exercises, including abstaining from self-destructive activities and attitudes, allocating personal resources in a godly manner and following simple rules of life, help to ***remind us that God is the center of each day.*** Such exercises produce stamina for continued acceptance of the Holy Spirit's invitation to "come and follow."

Following the leading of the Holy Spirit builds in us a growing capacity for extraordinary witness to God's kingdom, such as extending forgiveness where there has been genuine injury. It also reinforces in us the knowledge that *our new humanity in Jesus Christ is the work of the Spirit and not our own achievement.* In our human weakness, we need the strength and sustenance of the Holy Spirit to maintain the Godward direction of our life. Such assistance is clearly promised by Jesus: "When he, the Spirit of truth, comes, he will guide you into all truth" (John 16:13). This truth is what the author of Ephesians calls "the fullness of Christ" (Ephesians 4:13). The measure of this truth is nothing other than love. *Love is the first gift of the Spirit and the final test of our freedom in Jesus Christ* (see 1 Corinthians 13; Galatians 5:22; Colossians 1:8). All other marks of our new humanity—joy, peace, patience, kindness, generosity, faithfulness, self-control—are manifestations of this love, a love that binds us to Jesus Christ in the unity of the Holy Spirit for the sake of the world God loves so much. "Since we live by the Spirit, let us keep in step with the Spirit" (Galatians 5:25).

IN THE WORLD

In a life increasingly given to the guidance of the Holy Spirit, our new humanity in Jesus Christ gradually becomes more visible and effective in the world. Far from removing us from the messiness of the world, *spiritual formation plunges us into the middle of the world's rage and suffering.* It was to this place of pain and bewilderment that Jesus Christ was sent as the visible image of the invisible God (see John 14:9; Colossians 1:15). It was to this place of bitterness and infirmity that Jesus Christ was sent, not to condemn but to save (see John 3:17). Those who are being formed in his image take the same path. Love, the full measure of Christian maturity, impels us with kindly urgency in this direction. *Love desires to be seen, known and received, for by these actions it grows wider and deeper.* Through us love is extended to the furthest recesses of human sorrow and need. Thus, God's love for the world—in us because we are in Jesus Christ—becomes a sign of hope and a source of transformation in the world.

"No one is richer, no one more powerful, no one more free," observed Thomas à Kempis, "than *the person who can give his whole life to God and freely serve others with deep humility and love.*" To embody in thought, word and deed the love of God made known in our Lord Jesus Christ is the signal mark of faithful discipleship, the inexhaustible strength of vital congregations and the ultimate goal of spiritual formation.

—JOHN MOGABGAB

Meeting God in

Service

TEN CHAIRS WERE pulled closely together in a circle, but we were all leaning forward to catch Mary Jean's words. She seldom spoke during our small-group meetings, yet this week she seemed eager to talk. She described the time she had spent working in a community center and the relentless problems of poverty, addiction, and abuse she had encountered there. Tears came to her eyes as she concluded, "I feel helpless as I look at these families and see their suffering. What does God expect of me? How can I make a difference?"

Like Mary Jean, we may struggle to see just how God acts in a world of great suffering. And when it comes to our own role, we often don't know where to begin or what God might be asking of us. We sometimes feel overwhelmed, and we want to turn away from the realities that surround us. Yet as we begin to serve others, we often find our hesitations fading. We discover that when we help others we encounter God. We meet God in the midst of our efforts. This can happen in several ways.

LEARNING TO LOOK

We learn to see God by opening our eyes and actively looking for opportunities to serve others. From the beginning of his ministry, *Jesus constantly stayed alert to people and their needs.* It was one reason why he came. Jesus read from the book of Isaiah in the synagogue at Nazareth, applying these words to himself:

"The Spirit of the Lord is upon me,
    because he has anointed me
        to bring good news to the poor.
He has sent me to proclaim release to the captives
    and recovery of sight for the blind,
to let the oppressed go free,
    to proclaim the year of the Lord's favor."—Luke 4:18-19

Every day as he traveled with his disciples Jesus healed and fed and loved people. A number of stories in the Gospels tell us that *Jesus acted because he was moved with compassion.* As painful as it must have been, *he did not turn aside from people's suffering.*

Jesus not only saw the sufferings of human beings but also became involved in people's suffering to heal and bring new life. The story of the widow of Nain in Luke 7:11-17 illustrates this. As Jesus travels with his disciples and a crowd of followers, he encounters a funeral procession. The widow, he discovers, has lost her only son. Jesus sees her grief with eyes of compassion, knowing that as a widow she has been completely dependent on her son. Now she has no one—and nothing. Jesus says to her, "Do not weep," and raises the young man back to life. Then we find the words, "Jesus gave him to his mother" (v. 15). What compassion and mercy are captured in those words!

Again and again Jesus actively seeks the sick and needy. He goes directly to them; he notices their pain and suffering and responds with divine grace and love. *The common activities of his life—travels, conversations, seemingly chance meetings with people—become the settings for expressions of his caring alertness.* He appropriately perceives himself as a servant of God, and in serving God he ministers to those God loves.

LEARNING TO LISTEN

In the Gospel of John, Jesus demonstrates that this open-eyed attitude of caring was not to be confined only to his own ministry but was to characterize his followers' lives as well. *Jesus washed the disciples' feet as they gathered to celebrate the feast of the Passover, in part to remind us of our proper posture before others:* "You call me Teacher and Lord—and you are right, for that is what I am. So if I, your Lord and Teacher, have washed your feet, you also ought to wash one another's feet" (John 13:13-14). Not only do we open our eyes to need; we also listen to those we serve. We cannot know how to help others if we simply barge in to "fix" a list of problems we think we see in them. *We are to serve others with gentle openness and with a willingness to relinquish our own agenda.* We listen to their ideas and hopes and longings.

To listen requires a quieting of our own interests and experiences so that we can become open not only in that particular relationship but also to the ways in which God is present in the relationship. Henri J. M. Nouwen writes, "Real training for service asks for a hard and often painful process of self-emptying. The main problem of service is to be the way without being 'in the way.'"

Learning to become more open to others teaches us many things. *Openness cultivates in us an attitude of honesty.* We see ourselves, as well as others, more clearly. Then we are able to open ourselves to God—to let the Great Healer have those parts of us that are wounded and in need of healing and forgiveness. Just as we speak of God's love for and forgiveness of others, so we can claim that healing in our own lives.

Our lives may be deeply changed as we serve others. *As those we serve share their own pilgrimages, we see how God has been a part of their experiences.* Their vision of God may enlarge ours. Their words, feelings and desires may challenge us in surprising ways. When twentieth-century spiritual writer Evelyn Underhill went to Baron von Hügel for guidance about her relationship with God, he recommended that she spend a designated amount of time each week directly serving the poor so as to break open her heart to the needs of people and open her up more fully to experience God's grace. As a result she met a woman named Laura Rose, the beginning of a relationship that was to become deeply significant for Underhill's spiritual growth.

LEARNING TO LOVE

To looking and listening we add loving—of the most radical, sacrificial kind. It is easy to be captured by our own special interests and by self-absorption. *When we follow Jesus, however, normal priorities get turned upside down.* We confront what German pastor and theologian Dietrich Bonhoeffer called "the cost of discipleship."

God thereby transforms our self-interest into a new awareness of our interdependence. We identify the ways in which we need one another in order to grow in faithfulness. We find a new identity by centering our lives in the One who is the light of the world and who calls us to let our lights "shine before others, that they may see your good works and give glory to [our] Father in heaven" (Matt. 5:16). We realize that nothing matters more than bringing people to Jesus for healing and salvation.

Little by little our hearts, which can so easily become hardened to the needs of others, are changed into caring and compassionate hearts. Thomas Kelly, in his book, *A Testament of Devotion*, captures this phenomenon in these words: "God plucks the world out of our hearts, loosening the chains of attachment. And . . . hurls the world into our hearts, where we and [God] together carry it in infinitely tender love."

RESOURCES TO GET US THROUGH

The radical call to service does not pose for us an impossible duty, however. ***God promises to give us the power and resources we need*** through the indwelling spirit of Jesus. Paul wrote to the new converts in the first-century church in Corinth to remind them of their calling. Paul pointed out that he had come to them in weakness, fear and trembling, but that God had used him to demonstrate the power of the Spirit (see 1 Corinthians 1:18-31; 2:6-13). What freedom there is in knowing that God can use us in spite of our weaknesses!

Indeed, power is released through our vulnerability. ***It is through our vulnerabilities that we learn the nature of God's sufficiency.*** The only way we can confront head-on the pain of a suffering world is through utter reliance on God's grace. We can take to heart God's word to Paul, "My grace is sufficient for you, for power is made perfect in weakness" (2 Cor. 12:9).

Jesus is inviting us to love the world as he loves. Paul encouraged a congregation of Christians who were undergoing much struggle by reminding them that they were a letter of Christ, written not with ink but with the Spirit of the living God (2 Corinthians 3:2-3). What a word of promise for today! ***We go in the power of the Spirit.*** The Spirit speaks in and through what we do.

"Christian ministry," writes James Fenhagen, "is more than doing good. Ministry is an act of service performed either consciously or unconsciously in the name of Christ. Ministry is Jesus Christ expressing his life through us." ***When we are tempted to run and hide because the needs of the world are overwhelming and we feel helpless to make a difference, we can remember that we do not go alone.*** We venture out boldly, not because we underestimate or devalue the needs and woundedness of others but because we trust in the steadfast and abiding love of God.

In serving the needs of others in society, we meet God. We find joy, as Brother Lawrence found centuries ago, "doing little things for the love of God." And as we grow, we learn more about the love of Jesus and what it means to share it with others. This prayer in Ephesians describes what it means to mature in our relationship with Jesus: "I pray that, according to the riches of his glory, [God] may grant that you may be strengthened in your inner being with power through his Spirit, and that Christ may dwell in your hearts through faith, as you are being rooted and grounded in love" (Eph. 3:16-17).

—JANICE T. GRANA

Meeting God in

Everyday Life

"WE LIVE LIVES OF LITTLE THINGS," someone once said. We are occupied most often with the details of ordinary life. Driving to the office or factory, putting supper on the table, taking feverish kids to the doctor—these are the things that fill our hours. When we meet God, that encounter often takes place in and through everyday circumstances. Growing spiritually will mean "living to God on common occasions," as Horace Bushnell expressed it. Inevitably we cultivate our spiritual lives not just in quiet solitude but in the activity of everyday life. *We realize that God speaks to us not just in sky-rending revelations but also in the intimacy of quiet conversation* with our spouse, the freshness of a child's spontaneous observation, the warmth of a bubbling pot of chili, the comfort of a family-night ritual.

How do we meet God in the midst of our stressful, busy lives? How do we recognize the signs that, in Avery Brooke's wonderful phrase, lie "hidden in plain sight"?

Two intentions will help us.

REMEMBER GOD'S DEEDS

The Bible leaves no doubt that *God works through the inner and outer details of our everyday lives.* And if God is present in such moments, we cannot let them slide into oblivion:

"Take care and watch yourselves closely, so as neither to forget the things that your eyes have seen nor to let them slip from your mind all the days of your life" (Deut. 4:9). The psalmist, recalling God's careful involvement in Israel's history, vowed, "I will call to mind the deeds of the LORD; I will remember your wonders of old" (Ps. 77:11).

The act of remembering helped the people of Israel to keep events from the past vital in the present. Just as we pull out a photo album on a rainy day in order to recall the significant moments of our lives—to review the snapshots of graduations and confirmations, visits and vacations—so God wanted the people of Israel to keep their holy history vividly present in their minds. And they were to remember God's good deeds corporately, as a people. Recollection was a community event. As they gathered in various ways, the people recalled aloud the moments that had given them identity as people of God—when God led them to freedom from Egyptian bondage, gave them commandments and instruction, gave them life. "Remember the former things of old," Isaiah enjoined the people, speaking on God's behalf (Isaiah 46:9). *The Israelites' very identity depended on the God who had acted in their history.* To forget God's acts would have meant to forget that God had called and chosen them.

God's call to remember carried over into New Testament times. *Jesus urged his followers to recall God's work of redemption in his own life, death, and resurrection.* "Do this in remembrance of me," Jesus said at the Last Supper (Luke 22:19). Communion, in which we partake of the bread and the cup, is a supreme act of remembering. We also meet God through recalling what he has done for us personally. With David the psalmist we make certain that we "do not forget all [God's] benefits" in our daily lives (Psalm 103:2). To jog his readers' memories, David then recited specific benefits. He was not indulging in nostalgia but was gleaning from the past all that the Lord did and said. *When we remember the Lord's deeds, we likewise keep in the forefront of our minds what God has already shown us; we live in continuity with the events that have shaped us.* We recall the blessings of last year and the hardships of last week, remembering how God walked beside us and sometimes carried us in our moments of weakness and woundedness.

Conscious recollection requires discipline. In our live-for-the-moment culture, we may find the act of remembering more difficult than ancient people did. We are prone to become distracted by the details of the moment. We forget to "read life backward." But *memory can be a powerful resource for keeping our spiritual perspective alive.*

One practical aid to this holy remembering is keeping a journal. Many find it helpful to jot down prayers, record insights from Bible readings or put on paper the events that seem to be leading somewhere—events that have left an impression on them. ***Keeping a journal can be done in a way that meets your own needs and preferences.*** Journaling need not be an elaborate affair or something you slavishly perform every day. It can be as simple as you wish and as occasional as meets your need. If you have never used a journal, try taking a blank bound book, a spiral notebook or a binder full of paper—and then simply write. ***Make your writing an act of sanctified listening.*** When you write down your thoughts and ideas and emotions, they take definition and shape. You may find that as you write, you begin to untangle your confusion about what you are hearing from God. ***You may hear God speaking in ways in which you may not have been attentive otherwise.***

Do not allow yourself to relegate to a fuzzy memory the significant things going on within and around you. "The simplest ink," says an old Chinese proverb, "is more ***reliable than the finest mind." Writing becomes a way to extract a deeper meaning from what has happened to you.*** It becomes an act of remembering.

Leaf back through your journal pages every few weeks. ***Notice how God's purposes seem to be emerging in what has happened—and in what hasn't happened.*** Thank God for prayers that have been answered. Continue to lift up to God themes that emerge from what you've written, themes that reveal your heart's desires. And ***watch for a greater sense of personal direction.*** Keeping a journal, wrote Ronald Klug, is "like walking into a messy room—toys and clothes and books piled around—and slowly picking things up and putting them in their right places again. The room 'feels good' and I can go on living there. In a similar way, my journal helps me sort out things in my life and restore some internal order."

We can practice the art of remembering when we meet with family and friends. Conversations at family reunions might move beyond talk of sports or vacations to reflections about how God has proven faithful in our family's past and present stories. And when we go to church, worship can be an exercise in remembering. Spiritual growth groups, church school classes—any gathering of believers—can be an occasion to track God's actions in our midst. We recall all the ways God has been faithful. ***We "testify." And as we do, we find ourselves reminded of who God is through what he has done.***

REFLECT ON GOD'S DEEDS

Reflection—alert awareness of what is happening now—returns us to the present moment. ***Open-eyed reflection allows us to see God's hand at work or grasp insights we might otherwise have been too busy to notice.*** The Bible sometimes uses the word *meditation* for this kind of thoughtful reflection. We are not talking about the meditation of Eastern religions nor a privatized, overly individualistic quest for religious experience. Biblical meditation is always God-centered. It often focuses on God's Word revealed in scripture. And it often has to do with God's activity. "On your wondrous works I will meditate," the psalmist exults in Psalm 145:5. Just three verses earlier he had vowed, "Every day I will praise you." *An awareness of what God is doing and the impulse to praise God go hand in hand.*

Events of daily life therefore belong in our daily prayers. In the Lord's Prayer Jesus directed us to pray for God's will to be done on earth, not just in heaven—which means in our everyday lives as well. Knowing how much daily matters affect us, Jesus even encouraged his followers to pray for "daily bread"—the everyday sustenance that keeps our physical bodies going. *The likelihood that Jesus worked as a carpenter during his early adult years implies that God, through Jesus Christ's incarnation, has for all time graced daily work.* And God notices when "bad" things happen and operates through events so that, as the apostle Paul wrote, "we know in all things work together for good for those who love God" (Rom. 8:28). *All the realities of life, then, constitute the grist for our conversations with God.*

As we pray about our life experiences, we will begin to cultivate a spiritual alertness. Jean-Pierre de Caussade wrote of "the sacrament of the present moment." He meant that the very place where we are, the very things that we do, can mediate God's presence. Writing of Mary and Joseph, Jesus' parents, de Caussade asks, "What do they discern beneath the seemingly everyday events which occupy them? What is seen is similar to what happens to the rest of [hu]mankind. But what is unseen, that which faith discovers and unravels, is nothing less than God fulfilling [God's] mighty purpose. . . . God reveals himself to the humble in small things."

This reflection can take place in the workplace, where many of us spend much of our time. Martin Luther, one of the prime figures of the Protestant Reformation, argued that not just priest or nun, but also milkmaid or blacksmith, could become deeply conscious of God's presence. This can happen in our family times and during our leisure times. *Thomas Kelly writes, "a life of little whispered words of adoration, of praise, of prayer, of worship can be breathed all through the day."*

Staying alert to God's presence may be as simple as pausing to acknowledge that God is near. It may mean taking a few moments to pray during a lunch hour or coffee break. It may mean occasionally looking out the window to drink in the beauty of God's creation or really paying attention to the people with whom we live. And it certainly means *allowing everyday blessings—a sunset, a smile from a friend—to remind us of God and point us back to the Divine in gratitude.*

—TIMOTHY JONES

Meeting God in

Scripture

IN EVERY ERA, in myriad places, and in all kinds of circumstances, people have testified that the Bible speaks powerfully—that the Word of God can and does change lives. But perhaps you feel that your own experience with reading the Bible pales in significance when compared to such a standard. You feel like the woman who confessed, ***"Surely there has to be a way to get more out of my Bible reading!"*** Your times with the Bible yield much of value and interest—but transformation? That is another matter. You learn facts—places and names—but have yet to hear God's voice. As much as you value the insights gained, you long to meet God.

When you read and study scripture *it is possible to grow beyond an intellectual knowledge of the Bible to the transformation of your heart.* The Bible can become "a lamp to [your] feet and a light for [your] path" (Ps. 119:105). You can go to the heart of the matter and meet the Author. The eighteenth-century bishop Tikhon of Zodonsk articulated well what can happen: "Whenever you read the Gospel," he wrote, "Christ Himself is speaking to you. And while you read, you are praying and talking to Him." Reading and studying the Bible can become more fulfilling than anything you have previously experienced.

But how? Providentially we are heirs to several helpful approaches. The great spiritual writers of the past have given us a legacy that engages mind and heart, intellect and will. They have suggested ways that help us derive life from the text and so become agents of life for others.

In the history of Christian spirituality, the oldest and best-known approach to Bible reading is called "spiritual reading" or "divine reading" (the Latin is *lectio divina*). The practice dates back to at least the fourth century, but the idea behind it is even more ancient. Spiritual reading entails a fourfold approach:

First, read slowly. Choose a relatively short passage of a biblical book (no more than several paragraphs or a short chapter), and read meditatively, prayerfully. In this phase you are a seeker looking for the "word within the Word." ***Watch for a key phrase or word that jumps out at you*** or promises to have special meaning for you. Concern yourself not so much with the amount you are reading as the depth with which you read. It is better to dwell profoundly on one word or phrase than to skim the surface of several chapters. ***Read with your own life and choices in view,*** recalling Paul's injunction that God's word is "useful for teaching, for reproof, for correction, and for training in righteousness" (2 Tim. 3:16).

Second, meditate. Christian meditation is not stream of consciousness or free association, nor is it Eastern transcendental meditation. Rather, ***it is letting a special word or phrase that you discovered in the first phase of reading sink into your heart.*** It is what the biblical writers had in mind when they spoke of "meditating" on the Book of the Law "day and night" (Josh. 1:8; Ps. 1:2). For example, when you are reading Psalm 23, perhaps you linger at the phrase, "The LORD is my shepherd." For reasons that may not be immediately apparent, the word *my* stands out. You are struck by the idea that God can be—and wants to be—your shepherd. In this second phase of spiritual reading, stay with that thought. Use whatever study skills and related materials that are available to you to enrich your reflection. ***Bring mind, will, and emotions to the enterprise.*** This meditative stage is comparable to walking around a great statue, viewing it from multiple vantage points. You are like Mary, Jesus' mother, who heard of the angel's announcement and "treasured up" and "pondered" what she had heard (Luke 2:19).

Third, pray the text. You have listened; now you respond—that is, ***you form a prayer that expresses your response to the idea.*** You "pray it back to God." You are, in effect, engaging God in dialogue. In the case of "The LORD is my shepherd," your response could easily be a prayer of gratitude. It might be a prolonged recollection of all of the ways that

God has been present with you over the years, shepherding you through life. This phase of divine reading is in reality not separate from the other aspects but flows through all of them, so that *you are continually converting the text into a prayer*, a prayer formed by God's revealed will. What you have read is woven through what you tell God. You thereby acknowledge that God's Word "shall not return . . . empty, but it shall accomplish that which [God desires]" (Isa. 55:11).

Fourth, contemplate. That is, rest. In divine reading you eventually arrive at the place at which you no longer work on the text but allow it to work itself into you. *You let it soak into your deepest being.* You are not straining for additional insights; you simply are savoring an encounter—with God's truth and with God's own self. You enjoy the rest that Jesus promised those who come to him (see Matthew 11:28). Quietly, when ready, move toward the moment in which you *ask God to show you how to live out what you have experienced.*

Spiritual reading enables God to "speak and show" in ways that transform the written word into a living Word—just for you. Then, having "taste[d] and see[n] that the Lord is good" (Psalm 34:8), *you move outward in daily living to become a blessing to others*.

IGNATIAN READING

Attributed to Ignatius of Loyola (1491–1556) and articulated in his "Spiritual Exercises," the Ignatian method of reading the Bible likewise invites us to enter actively and fully into the text. *It encourages detachment from either ego-driven success or fear-motivated anxiety*, leaving the soul free to obey God's stirrings.

Generally, Ignatian reading works best with narrative material in which actual characters lived a story of faith. The idea is to *place yourself into the text as a careful observer*—a "fly on the wall," if you will. Ignatius commended the use of the five senses in such meditation. You taste, hear, see, smell, and feel your way through the passage. Occasionally you become one of the characters, seeing the story unfold from his or her viewpoint. Most of all, the aim is to help you *perceive the narrative from the viewpoint of Jesus so that you may more fully participate in his mind, heart, and work.*

For the sake of practice, you might like to concentrate on John 18:1-11 and spend five days reading it. Each day, imagine yourself as a different one of the characters: Judas, a soldier, Peter, the high priest's servant, or Jesus. As you enter vicariously into the position of each character, *ask God to teach you how to live in greater fidelity and obedience*—which is the ultimate aim of the Ignatian method of reading scripture and of Ignatian spirituality in general.

FRANCISCAN READING

While not a direct by-product of the teachings of Francis of Assisi, Franciscan reading exhibits primary qualities of Franciscan spirituality, such as action, spontaneity, love, praise, beauty, and delight in creation. Like Ignatian reflection, Franciscan reading involves the mental process of entering personally into the text. But this method is more fluid. *It allows the encounter with God to incorporate ordinary activities and daily experiences.*

For example, turn in your Bible to Isaiah 53 and read through this chapter. To help you enter into its message and reflect on Jesus' sacrificial death on the cross, the Franciscan method would invite you to take actions such as these: If you have a model of a cross with Jesus on it, you might hold it in your hand, gazing at the details of the Lord's crucified body. You might sing a hymn such as "O Sacred Head, Now Wounded" or "The Old Rugged Cross." You might look through today's newspaper and identify places in the world where people are suffering. You might write a poem or paint a picture to capture what you are thinking and feeling. In the Franciscan spirit, you would express your emotions through an activity. You would be encouraged to "feel" something of what Jesus experienced on your behalf. You would saturate the entire experience with prayer, *asking God to make you an instrument of peace* in the lives of those who are suffering.

To be sure, these methods do not exhaust our options for formative reading. You might use the fruit of the Spirit described in Galatians 5:22-23 as a lens through which you read, asking yourself how a particular passage might deepen love, joy, peace, patience, kindness, goodness, gentleness, faithfulness, and self-control in your life. You might use what some have called the Fivefold Question (What does this passage say about God's nature? What does it say about human nature? What does it say about how God relates to people? What does it suggest about how I might pray? What does it suggest about how I might act?).

Whatever method you use at any given time, adopt an underlying attitude of openness to seeking truth. We pray for a "scriptural mind" that is obedient, faithful to the historic Christian tradition, Christ-centered and personal. *We must desire to find truth and be willing to apply it to our own lives* and our relationships with others. Apart from such foundational commitments, any method becomes mere technique. With them, any of the methods of reading scripture can become a true means of grace.

—J. Steven Harper

About the Author

Anne Crumpler

Anne Crumpler comes from a long line of preachers, teachers, and writers; she learned theology, Bible, and English grammar over the dinner table. She also has a Bachelor of Arts in Philosophy from Chatham College and a Master of Religious Education from St. Meinrad School of Theology.

Anne has been an assistant editor in the Department of Youth Publications, the United Methodist Publishing House. She is presently a freelance writer and editor.

Anne is a contract editor for *The Upper Room* daily devotional guide and for *Devozine*. She has written Bible lessons for *Mature Years* and *Daily Bible Studies*, commentary for *The New International Lesson Annual*, articles for *Devozine* and *Alive Now*, devotions for *The Upper Room Disciplines* and *365 Meditations for Families*, sermon helps for *What Difference Would It Make?* (a program of The Upper Room), study guides for Lent and Advent offered online by The Upper Room, and lessons on the kingdom of God for volume three of *The Pastor's Bible Study*.

Anne lives in Nashville, Tennessee, with her husband, David. They have two spectacular children, Rachel and Benjamin.